THE BABY BOND

How to Raise
An Emotionally
Healthy Child

Dianna Hine

Cocoon Books

Prescott, Arizona

Disclaimer

This book is meant to serve as a source of information. It is not a replacement for professional help and advice. Neither the author nor Cocoon Books can be responsible for the decisions of the reader based on the interpretation of information found in this book. If the reader does not want to be held to this disclaimer, Cocoon Books will be glad to refund the cost of the book upon its return.

Published by Cocoon Books
303 East Gurley Street
Prescott, Arizona 86301
(520) 636-9626

Publisher's Cataloging-in-Publication Data

Hine, Dianna.
The Baby Bond: How to Raise an Emotionally Healthy Child/by Dianna Hine. —1st ed.
p. cm.
Includes bibliographical references and index.
Preassigned Library of Congress Catalog Card Number 98-092462
ISBN: 1-891974-00-9
1. Parent and infant. 2. Infant psychology.
3. Attachment behavior in children. I. Title.
Printed in the United States of America

Cover Design/Book Design: The Agrell Group
Cover Photo: © Digital Vision

This book
is dedicated to parents,
who do the most
important job there is,
with very little help.

PART ONE

Bonding

In the Beginning...

Imagine that you are floating on the warm waters of the Caribbean, the gentle waves lulling you to sleep. The temperature is perfect. The sounds of birds and breeze soothe you. Your every need is tended to and you feel totally safe and serene. All is well and you haven't a care in the world.

Then suddenly you are dropped into the middle of Tokyo, Japan and confronted with a blasting confusion. Movement surrounds you, sounds invade you. You're helpless, afraid and cry out for help, but no one understands you.

That's what it's like to be born. One minute you're in paradise, the next you're in the great unknown, lying on your back.

In a single jolt, babies go from the weightless sanctuary of a cozy womb to what for them is a different planetary system altogether. In a breath and a heartbeat they have to adjust, going from a wet universe to a dry one, from living in darkness to being greeted by fluorescent lights, hearing once muted sounds now become amplified, and contending with completely new experiences—like gravity and breathing through lungs. Imagine never knowing anything but the soft caresses of your pouch and your first out-of-womb sensation is that of being rammed by contractions. You've never been touched by anything but your watery nest and suddenly busy nurses whisk you from womb to examining table to suction fluids out of your nose and mouth, and apply drops to your eyes. You are weighed and measured, flown from one room to another, your foot is stuck with a pin—and sometimes an oxygen mask is put over your face, all in the first hour of life (and that's if everything has gone well). One wonders how any of us survive the stress of being born.

We survive because miraculous physiological and behavioral systems are in place that have evolved over thousands of years and that assist in the survival of our species. For example, hormones are released in babies during the delivery process that alleviate the swelling and soft tissue trauma caused by being pushed and pulled through the birth canal. Even labor is a useful piece of engineering. The squeezing that infants experience forces amniotic fluid out of their lungs and helps prepare them for the challenge of breathing on their own. In addition, the auditory, cognitive, and nervous systems have been left under construction, a condition that protects newborns from sensory overload. And to further cushion their shock, babies receive tranquilizing hormones from mother's breast milk and are soothed by hearing the familiar sound of her heartbeat when they nurse. The list of safeguards nature has provided for newborns is extensive. Countless strategies with a complex set of checks and balances have been designed to protect them from the natural, and sometimes unnatural, calamities of birth.

But this is nothing new. All of nature is a delicate balance of dancing cells, molecules and genes, organized into interdependent systems designed to survive as life structures. From bacteria to Beluga whales, from jungle ecosystems to the workings of the human body, living matter is made up of a network of partnerships put together just so. The complexity of this many relationships is difficult to grasp. The numbers of possible combinations and collisions are in the realm of the unfathomable. With the consequences of one function affecting the other, it is mind boggling that so many organizations, from the cellular level on up, can work together so magnificently. Somehow they blend to create one huge working community of choreographed parts.

What every living system has in common is interdependency. We are interrelated links that make a chain of DNA possible. We are jigsaw pieces that together create a picture, a life. The framework that defines a state of health is preserved by a composition of elements, placed like a house of cards. But pull out too many necessary ingredients and the structure weakens and sometimes fails. The secret of what makes us a nexus of matter that grows and thrives is embodied within the laws, rules, and regulations that govern creation.

Clues to understanding the natural laws that influence human beings are, in part, encoded in the adaptations that were selected into our gene pool long ago. Those adaptations were made in response to the environment into which we were born and the limitations it has imposed on us. We have been shaped by the conditions that exist on this planet. We have been living on this world, depending on it for our survival for millennia. We have had to make adjustments in order to coexist with it and each other, and these circumstances have molded us into who we are today.

In order to correctly interpret what makes us tick, we need to understand the motivations behind those adaptations. What is the rhyme or reason of why we have developed certain traits and tendencies, likes and dislikes, universal needs that leave us feeling horrible if dissatisfied? What is it that nature requires we do in order to feel healthy?

We have uncovered many of the rules for our physiological health, but what is essential for our *psychological* fitness? Unraveling the whole puzzle of the mind is difficult because it is so easy to lose sight of what ties all the pieces together. Endless combinations of cause and effect make discerning the roots of emotional and behavioral imbalances troublesome. Discovering the mystery of the human psyche is more intriguing than figuring out a Sherlock Holmes novel. There's much that can be gathered as evidence (symptoms), but deciphering where they came from (etiology) often remains an enigma.

Part of unraveling the secrets of our psychology begins with understanding the evolutionary purpose it serves. How do anger and fear increase our chances of survival? What good is guilt? Why isn't compassion a built-in feature? If our emotions are meant to help us, why do they seem to get in our way more than add to our chances? Or, do they really get in our way? How do our thoughts, feeling and behaviors develop and what is required to begin the process of growing an emotionally healthy human being? These are some of the questions this book will address.

Nature's Plan

Though infants are somewhat protected during labor and delivery, there is a limit to the range of circumstances they are prepared to face not only at birth but thereafter. There are laws that govern their physiological and psychological health, and there is a price to be paid for breaking them. Human beings are at the mercy of certain **species-specific needs** and going outside those prescribed boundaries leaves us open to a great expanse of potential hazards.

We don't question the requirements—a baby has to eat, sleep, and breathe because the outcome of not meeting these needs is clear—certain death. But other mandates are not nearly as distinct—it took many centuries for modern humans to fully realize that if one never holds a baby death can also result. The emotions don't bleed, they don't have a location, they can't be poked and prodded. We haven't been sure until recently what some of the defining rules are that foster our psychological health.

An historical view of childhood

Over the last several hundred years though, we've certainly guessed at what they were. In the Middle Ages most babies did not live to see their first birthday. It was probably an automatic defense for parents not to grow too fond of their children so as not to grieve their loss. Perhaps as a result, the children who did live were not treated very well. They were considered property and had no claim to emotional or physical well-being. Their sole purpose was to support the survival of the family. In the 18th century, children had perhaps a few more rights but were still considered much less deserving than adults. By the 19th century, children were cherished more but were considered to be uncivilized. They had to be taught to fit into polite society before they could earn much respect. Repressing a child's unruly behavior required instruction and education. Though the introduction of schools took some children out of the factories and the fields, it deposited them into the mine field of discipline and grooming.

Standards in parenting practices took another turn in the early 1930's. The experiments of John Watson put *behaviorism* on the map as the key to proper parenting and it continues to be a major force today. Watson and others in the field convinced us that the best way to produce well-behaved children was to train them through the regulation of stimulus and response. Desirable behaviors that were rewarded would thrive and undesirable behaviors, if ignored, would be extinguished.

As a result parents today almost unthinkingly believe their children's complaints are not to be trusted and that their demands and behavior require shaping. Children are basically thought to be bottomless pits of desire who, if indulged, will become demanding, out of control brats. Parents have been led to believe that if they are too permissive they will "spoil" their children.

Until fairly recently, most advice given to parents was based on the assumption that babies don't know much and parents always know what is best. Fusses and cries were sometimes thought to be reasonable requests for food or comfort, but not always. Their communications were viewed with suspicion. Is this cry a manipulation to be indulged and coddled? Should I pick up my baby this time or is she asking for simply too much attention? We have been told for decades to reinterpret our baby's needs and instead of responding to them, do what we think is best. Parents have had to anticipate which responses would mold their children into considerate, reasonable, and obedient children and which would "spoil" them.

However, child development experts have discovered that a well-behaved child is not necessarily an emotionally healthy one. A child's species-specific needs cannot be conditioned away.

What science tells us

How can we be sure that we now understand what babies need to be emotionally, socially and intellectually healthy? For one, scientists have the ability to study pictures of an infant's developing brain through the use of imaging scans. Advances in medical technologies have expanded our ability to observe and understand just how a human being is put together.

One of the more recent and startling discoveries–at birth a newborn's brain is nothing more than a mass of short circuits. The majority of the networks needed to pull the brain into working order haven't evolved yet.

This single discovery significantly changes the way we view infant development. First and foremost it means that a baby's early experiences are the architects of his brain—the vehicle of thought and feeling. That's because the brain grows its networks and synaptic connections in response to becoming stimulated. The patterns of experience, or sensations and emotions a baby has that are *consistently repeated*, will dictate the manner in which his brain circuitry forms.

Since an infant's brain is still evolving, scientists can study the effects of specific child rearing practices or childhood experiences. They are able to begin answering the question: what causes a baby's brain to develop growth-producing circuitry and which experiences result in a lack of development or unhealthy growth patterns?

What they have found is that healthy patterns of development result when babies are consistently and sensitively responded to. A tragic lack of circuitry, especially in the areas of the brain that regulate emotion and which are key to cognitive development, has been observed in children who have been neglected or abused.

A special Spring/Summer 1997 edition of Newsweek entitled "Your Child" reports on a number of the latest studies on infant brain development. A study conducted by Dr. Linda Mayes of the Yale Child Study Center concludes that repetitive fearful and stressful experiences shape how the brain is constructed. These types of experiences not only dictate how the brain becomes organized but can interfere with the kind of development important to learning.

Dr. Bruce Perry, neurobiologist and assistant professor at the Baylor College of Medicine, has found that children whose home life is unpredictable, unsafe, abusive and neglectful, grow brains especially designed to survive in those conditions. The synapses to form in the first three years of life correspond with the demands being made of the child. If infants or toddlers feel afraid, uncertain, distressed, or in pain for the majority of their day, their brains will be tailor made for doing battle and fleeing danger. This type of development might be useful if we still had to guard against predators and wage war against our enemies, but it is detrimental for the child who grows up in a society based on cooperation and interdependency.

Dr. Perry and others have observed that the brains of abused and neglected children are 20-30% smaller than normal. One explanation to account for this phenomenon is found in a substance called cortisol. Powerful stress hormones, including cortisol, are released in the brain in response to trauma and are so potent they can damage and destroy brain cells. One can actually see in imaging scans dark holes of inactivity in the brains of abused and neglected children. The destruction is clearly visible.

The centers that tend to be targeted by this assault happen to correspond with the higher brain functions: thinking, memory, impulse control, and the emotions. On the other hand, the centers of the brain that become overemphasized in consistently stressed children tend to fall into the category of lower brain functions—instinct, arousal, and vigilance. Consistently frightened and traumatized infants and small children develop brains that are wired for danger.

Sadly, children emerging from these uncertain beginnings usually have a number of social problems and they are often blamed for behaving badly. They tend to be children who are over-reactive, impulsive, anxious, angry, and hypersensitive and their behaviors and reactions are usually inappropriate. But they are just following what comes naturally to them—reacting as they have been programmed to behave. For infants to be encouraged to develop traits such as thoughtfulness, cooperation, respect, and intellectual curiosity, they require a secure and consistently responsive environment.

One study directed by Megan Gunnar, a developmental psychologist from the University of Minnesota showed that a child's resilience to stress can be affected by how secure and safe the child feels with his caretaker. Children under two years old will normally have elevated levels of stress hormones when put in upsetting situations such as when they are vaccinated, separated from their mothers or in the presence of a stranger. But after two years of age, children who have a secure bond with their caretaker will no longer register this kind of distress with elevated levels of the stress hormones. The insecure child will.

The situation infants find the most frightening and distressing is when they don't trust their caretakers, either because they are unfamiliar with them or because the caretakers aren't responsive to them. However, there are other situations infants find distressing, such as when they are around repeated screaming and fighting, even if it's not being directed at them, or when they are cared for by a parent who is depressed and disengaged.

A six-year study was performed at the University of Washington, monitoring the brain waves of babies raised by depressed mothers. The study, conducted by Geraldine Dawson, revealed that the left frontal region of the brain, where many of our positive emotions reside, had greatly reduced activity, and the results were especially severe when the mother was also irritable and disengaged. These babies were not developing structures in the brain needed to experience joy. However, if the depression lifted before the child turned three years old, brain activity returned to normal.

Far from spoiling infants–responsive attention is what their brains need for healthy expansion.

Additionally, the strides that have been made in the last decade in the area of evolutionary science have helped us to understand who we are as a species. Evolution is a slow process which means that the adaptations we experience today are ones that were set into our lineage a long time ago. Who we are is essentially who we were many, many thousands of years ago. Genetically we are still hunters and gatherers. We are wired to survive the life we had back then, with all its dangers and uncertainties.

The survival tricks of a species develop through trial and error and can not be altered overnight. The short time our modern-day culture has existed is a blink of the eye in the course of human history. We can do little to reject our heritage. Even though we may not feel the same pressures and dangers our ancestors experienced, we are obliged to conform to the plan that has evolved–at least as it concerns infant care. To some extent a developed intelligence can counter some of the traits that exert their influence over us. Reasoning, knowledge and experience give us a certain amount of control over our programming. However, a baby doesn't have that option.

Even though human beings (including human babies) are adaptive, it is not a fool-proof system. We have automatic coping strategies and responses ready that are designed to counter threats to our survival. We are flexible and will do what we can to put up with whatever conditions we find ourselves in. But sometimes those adaptations end up doing us more harm than good. There is a limit to how much we are able to compensate. After a certain point, coping can be as damaging as it is helpful.

For instance, we've developed responses to fear that have allowed us to adapt to threatening situations. Adrenaline and other hormones are pumped through our bodies giving us a burst of energy to endure a threat. Blood moves from temporarily non-essential systems, like digestion, to the soon-to-be-challenged arms and legs. Breathing quickens, increasing the flow of oxygen to the muscles, and before you know it, we are ready to fight or flee disaster. However, too many stress hormones flooding our system on a daily basis over years can cause numerous diseases and disorders, as many people have discovered. High blood pressure and damaged organs tell us the fight or flight response has been forced to go too far. There is just so much stress a human being is equipped to endure.

As a thinking species we have the freedom to reason and decide a great number of our behaviors. We can attempt to forge almost any course we choose. And in doing so, we can stray from meeting some of our species-specific needs–and still survive. But survive in what condition? When do adaptations do more harm that good and become maladaptive?

Most animals get a lot of help from nature when it comes to parenting. They have built-in drives compelling them to behave in particular ways. For instance, mammals instinctually lick their young, for sometimes hours after the birth. To an outside observer this simply looks like a mother cleaning up a wet and bloody newborn. The licking, however, is what stimulates the newborn's nervous and respiratory systems to kick in, and growth hormones to circulate. If this programming wasn't in place, the species would perish.

An animal's young are also programmed with specific behaviors to maximize survival. Even though they may barely be able to walk or see, newborn mammals, except for humans, are able to wobble and drag themselves to the nearest nipple, latch on, and nurse soon after birth without any help. When mother goes out to hunt, they know to stay close to home, and when she moves on they are equipped to hold on or follow, without assistance. These behaviors are basically automatic and most mammalian young have at least this much maturity and self-reliance at birth, unlike human babies.

Human parents don't have the instinctive behaviors other animals have. We may be inclined to have nurturing feelings when our infants are born, but we don't have automatic responses telling us what to do. Humans have been blessed with intelligence and we have choices instead of strict codes of behavior to follow. Rather than nature showing us the way, we have been provided with guidelines. In theory, this arrangement should increase our chances for survival because we are able to improvise solutions when novel situations arise. But it also means there is more room for error. We can choose to ignore nature's plan for parenting and come up with completely new theories of our own—and that is exactly what we've done.

The wondrous systems we have developed

Nature's plan for optimal development can be deciphered by observing the traits and the biological, physiological and behavioral systems that we have evolved. Specifically, nature's plan for babies evolved in response to their greatest threat—an infant's absolute and complete helplessness. Babies can not take care of a single one of their essential needs. Someone has to feed, clothe, carry, and care for them with devotion and dedication, using up many of his or her own resources for years to come, or that infant will definitely die. No other animal is as unformed or takes as long to achieve independence as human babies. **Therefore, nothing is more important to the survival of a baby than a bond with a trusted caretaker.** That bond is the most important condition needed to ensure the survival of our species. Therefore, the traits most likely to develop would have been those that would have encouraged this bond between babies and their caretakers.

Researchers have discovered that in fact there are some ingenious mechanisms in place that do just that. For example, at birth, a baby's nearsighted vision blurs all the confusing movements and activities outside his immediate environment, but allows him to see a distance of 8 to 12 inches away—the same length as between breast and a mother's face. Babies are spared visual overload while being encouraged to focus on their mothers. And of all the possible objects that might vie for his attention, studies have shown that baby is programmed to prefer looking at the human face (in particular the mother's versus a stranger's) more than any other distraction.

This orchestration of directed sight in the breastfeeding position also promotes bonding with the mother. If anything is going to encourage a caregiver to stick around it is the wondrous gaze of a baby. Whether between parent and child or two lovers, when people look into each other's eyes, they feel a sense of connectedness.

It's also no accident that the breastfeeding position not only encourages a bond between mother and child, but is the perfect place for infants to hang out during much of their first few months because of the many benefits they receive. Every time they nurse, babies are visually stimulated by their mother's face, which in turn stimulates the brain. In addition, they experience security and therefore are not stressed. Not being overly stressed means they have more energy to put into growing instead of crying. Mental and physical development are also promoted by the sensation of touch, especially when it's skin to skin. And from breast milk, babies receive a constant stream of brain-building chemicals, tranquilizing hormones, natural antibiotics, and hormones that promote feelings of attachment.

And if all that weren't enough, listening to the mother's heartbeat and breathing helps the baby to regulate the erratic rhythm of his own systems. A baby focusing his vision on mother's interested face and tuning into her loving, melodic voice; feeling her stimulating touch while calmly orchestrating the sucking, breathing, and swallowing process of nursing; produce a harmonizing effect on baby's chaotic state.

Since infants are so helpless, their most important task is to communicate what they need, using whatever tools are at their disposal. Part of nature's plan is giving babies the ability to signal their caretaker to meet their species-specific needs. But since babies can't talk the only means they have to communicate with us is through emotion and gesture. They tell caretakers what is needed with displays of pain, fear, frustration, anger and withdrawal, or curiosity, contented smiles and gleeful chortles. The inclination built into parents is to respond. We are moved to try to interpret and answer their cues.

When we respond appropriately to their signals, babies feel successful, organized, and on the right track. When we don't respond, or respond inappropriately, infants feel defeated, ineffectual, confused, and unimportant. They feel the same way we might if we were forced to communicate with someone who didn't speak the same language. We would also be angry, frustrated and feel very impotent if our attempts at communicating were ignored.

Babies are the ones whose lives are at stake and they are very limited in what they can do by themselves to survive. Therefore, the few independent behaviors they are capable of are going to be very, very important. It is now widely accepted that when infants less than a year old cry, they aren't kidding. They are asking for what they *need*, not what they *want*. As they get older, babies will increasingly need opportunities to wrestle with autonomy, and will require less to be done for them. But most of their behavior will still reflect their need for security, stimulation, and comfort.

What we find babies programmed to ask for no matter what their race, creed, color, nationality, or economic situation is to be sensitively and consistently responded to by a trusted caretaker, because that is what they need to feel they will survive.

Some pretty effective strategies have evolved that will insure that this connection between parent and child takes place.

- Babies are cute, cuddly, and engaging, encouraging caretakers to pick them up and find them irresistible.
- They coo, smile, wiggle and squeal, delighting caretakers and giving them incentive to continue their devotion.
- Babies cry and make sounds that are impossible to ignore. These noises are annoying and work well to get someone's attention.
- Babies experience warnings in the form of pain and fear if they are not consistently and sensitively cared for. This signals them to cry louder, and cling longer.
- Because consistency is so important to their survival, babies are programmed to be agitated, even severely distressed if they don't *trust* their caretaker. Hopefully their continuous cries and whines will cause a caretaker to become more trustworthy (i.e. consistent).

In cases where babies have not had their needs met, they adapt to the deprivation and integrate it as their working model. If their stress is severe they will develop coping mechanisms that are maladaptive, but which protect them from experiencing too much pain, fear and neglect. For instance, they may learn to avoid their caretakers rather than rely on them for comfort. They may even learn how to detach themselves from their feelings of distress. However, these adjustments can create serious emotional consequences that can potentially follow a child into adulthood.

In many ways an infant's emotional development is fragile. As was true in utero, your baby needs a healthy environment in which to flourish. The umbilical cord to the womb may have been cut at birth, but emotionally and even physically, a parent still grows his or her baby for many months to come.

A baby's healthy development results from being sensitively and consistently responded to by one or a few trusted people. This *connection* is referred to as bonding and is the model for growing an emotionally healthy child.

The Effects of Mothers And Caretakers

So far I have referred to the "caretaker" as the person the baby has formed a bond with because it is not always the mother, and babies can have more than one person to whom they feel attached. However, the mother does have a special relationship with her baby. Together they've experienced the same body, the same activities and feelings for nine months. All sounds, emotions, movements, and responses have been shared by both. Soon after birth, babies can recognize the sound of their mother's voice and can distinguish the scent of her breast milk from another mother's. It also isn't long before a mother can recognize the sound of her own infant's cry–a sound so potent it has the power to "let down", or make available, her supply of breast milk. In addition, mothers have been supplied with certain chemicals (oxytocin and prolactin), which increase their ability to nurture, and which are released when mothers are nursing or holding their babies. All these are ingredients that help mothers feel securely bonded to their child. There is no denying that mothers have been given some extra accessories to assist in the healthy development of their infants.

It makes sense that the person chosen to be outfitted with an added survival kit, is also the person most likely to be there after the baby is born—the mother. Does that mean adoptive mothers or stay-at-home dads won't be able to be tuned in and build the same quality of bond with their babies? Absolutely not. Primary caretakers can and must form a bond with the baby, but the ideal situation is for babies to be breastfed and to be with their mothers. This doesn't mean women have to give up their careers or return to a life without choices. But, raising a child is a job too, one that we choose. We can't afford not to make parenting our first priority.

In order to set our priorities we must first decide what the goals are. Knowing what is optimal points us in the right direction and shows us what to aim for. Initially, the mother becoming the primary attachment figure is the best scenario, but not the only one that can work.

Sadly, many women can't stay home with their babies. Generally speaking, parenting is not valued by business and government the same way economic growth is. Most women simply can't afford to stay home with their infants. This situation is a travesty and ultimately must be changed, but in the meantime parents have to be very careful about who takes care of their babies and how. Whether grandma, dad, or daycare provider, the person who takes care of your child needs to offer the kind of sensitive and consistent care that encourages babies to become securely attached. Our comfort with frequently adopting substitute care for our babies is dangerous and a trend that is starting to reveal a dark side. Too often substitute care results in inadequate care for the baby.

Because a baby's brain is still forming and her awareness unfolding, early experiences, whether traumatic or growth producing, are literally being built into the ground floor of her neural network. The future of how or what she feels, and what she believes, will in part be shaped by whether or not she learns to trust others and feel valued. Being recorded into the brain's building blocks are her expectations of whether or not the world is a safe place and whether or not she can handle stressful situations successfully. A daycare provider who spends nine hours a day with your child is having a profound effect on what your child is incorporating as the basis of her self-esteem, her intellectual capabilities and her working models of well-being.

A baby's developing mental/emotional patterns and concepts are being laid down as a row of bricks would be, in relationship to each other and the foundation beneath. If the first layer isn't put down correctly, the second layer will conform to the mistake, and each succeeding layer will be skewed a little more. When a problem like this arises a mason can go back and rebuild— but people can't. They must heal. The more layers there are, the more difficult it is to remedy the problem. The longer these disturbances are left untreated, the greater the possibility the damage will be irreversible. The less secure the attachment in the first three years, the more likely it is that disturbances in the emotions will exist later in life.

The way the brain processes information and forms new circuitry is by becoming stimulated. Hearing, seeing, touching, moving, and feeling, prompt a baby's brain to register and respond to those experiences and, if necessary, grow more synaptic networks to handle the incoming information. This means that an infant's primary mode of learning is to ingest the models of experiences around her. When she is in pain and someone picks her up and soothes her, she is learning that she is competent and can make positive things happen. She is learning that she is important—worthy of love and attention. These concepts and feelings become part of her neural network.

Whatever babies are shown becomes a blueprint for future behavior. If you show your children kindness and respect, empathy and consideration, then that is what they are going to learn. How you treat your baby is going to influence his or her conclusions about the world.

If a baby receives inadequate care, then he or she learns the world is unpredictable, frightening, and not to be trusted. In response, she will develop mechanisms that will help her to feel safe and protected, such as avoiding attachments, becoming excessively controlling, and being defensive and covertly manipulative.

The Challenges of Parenting

"**P**ush—puuusshh, I can see the baby's head." Sweat drips down the woman's cheek. She groans but manages to pull herself up for one more round. "Puuush"—she yells to herself. "Come on body, you can do it." Then, just when she thinks she can't go on, the tremendous pressure disappears and someone shouts, "It's a boy!" In one amazing moment, she becomes a mother.

Giving birth is a profound experience—bringing you challenges and rewards unlike anything else—that is, except for parenting. How perfect that we have the experience of birth to provide us with previews of coming attractions. Becoming a mom or a dad is wondrous and difficult, fulfilling and draining. It's every experience you can imagine having—and more. Nothing can really prepare you for what's to come, for the exhilaration you'll feel when your child takes his first steps; the concern if, by a certain age, he hasn't; the joy of your baby's first smile; the worry when he won't stop crying. More than once in your career as a parent it will dawn on you, "I'm responsible for this helpless human being and he didn't come with an instruction manual."

Even with a manual, parenting is, at best, a never-ending stream of learning as you go along. You can seek out the best baby books, the most knowledgeable advice, you can learn everything there is to know about what foods to offer and how to toilet train, but no book will be tailor-made for your particular child. There is no such thing as the textbook baby. Some infants cry very little, others cry for hours every night. Your toddler may be of the easily distracted variety and her playmates the single-minded type. While rocking is usually a sure-fire baby calmer, your infant may not tolerate that much stimulation, preferring slow, gentle movements, low lighting and quiet rooms.

A common misconception is the belief that a strong-willed child should be remade into an easygoing one. A baby who lies quietly all day without fussing to be picked up is often labeled as the good one and a more demanding baby as bad. These children simply have different temperaments. The quiet baby still needs to be held and played with as much as the strong-willed child needs our patience and love; both are expressing their uniqueness. Your baby's temperament is what makes him or her special. Everybody comes into this world with a one-of-a-kind combination of traits and those that are less demanding are not necessarily more desirable. Some parents may get out of a little more work with the quieter child. But then again there may be an exuberance shared with the higher strung baby that isn't experienced with the more passive one.

Fussy, clingy, easily startled and agitated infants are trying, like all other babies, to get what they need to maintain their equilibrium. They are what authors of *The Baby Book*, Dr. William

Sears and his wife Martha Sears, RN, refer to as "high need" babies. They come into the world needing a lot of help and usually require more of everything: more patience and attention, more holding and soothing. These babies are intense by nature. Sometimes their parents feel like failures because they are unable to shape them into mellower beings. Many people view passionate displays as reflecting badly on parenting skills. Not true. A fussy or hypersensitive child is not necessarily an unhappy one. A baby's behavior is a combination of emotional well-being, physical health, and temperament.

Infants who are not well cared for may also act clingy, fussy, and anger easily, but there is a difference. They also avoid eye contact and don't soften when comforted. They are less secure in general. Nevertheless, both the high need and the insecure baby are signaling that they need something when they fuss and cry.

Whether or not they need a little or a lot, babies ask for what they lack to feel right. Some babies simply require more care.

Dr. Stanley Greenspan, pediatric psychiatrist from George Washington University explains that even though children are each born with their own unique temperament, it can be modified by how their parents respond to them. A child who is under-reactive to sounds and sensations may become even more withdrawn without the concerted effort of parents. A highly strung child could become less resistant and combative if disciplined with patience and talked to calmly. Temperament is not fixed but it does influence how parents and others may respond to their children. How a parent reacts can emphasize or modify naturally inherited traits.

Because each child is unique and changing all the time, parents need to be flexible. When your baby goes through a particularly difficult stage, it will be time to shift gears and get in sync with him all over again. Typically around 3 months, between 9 to

12 months, and again around 18 months, babies go through developmental shifts that can be challenging for them. For a while they may feel more insecure or frustrated. The baby you had been able to easily leave with the occasional babysitter, now finds strangers intolerable. He used to stay asleep until early morning; now he wakes up three to four times a night. You wonder what to do, why this is happening.

If your baby cries to be held and you are drawn to pick her up, then trust your instincts. Your intuition is pulling at you for a reason. You can sense your child's very real fear and discomfort. If you put her down and she cries frantically, you're probably not going to feel good about leaving her. At other times you may sense your baby needs to be put down for a few moments and given a chance to settle into sleep. Her cries are half-hearted and you don't sense your child feeling abandoned or insecure. Your intuition provides you with the guidance to know how and when to meet your child's needs for security.

Until your baby is at least a year old, he will be communicating *only* what is essential, and you can trust the information. Your infant is programmed to only ask for what he needs—what he must have to flourish. Physical imbalances can disturb a baby's ability to convey reliable information, but excluding the intrusion of medical problems, basic instincts and urges are designed to guide an infant's behaviors. He knows to get help whenever he is afraid, bored, uncomfortable or in pain, because those experiences indicate a threat to his survival. If your child is very afraid and distressed every time you leave him, he is telling you, "This fear is not manageable." His built-in survival programming kicks in and he feels, "If I am not with you, I'll perish. I haven't experienced enough safety to risk this separation." A very angry infant may be telling you he's in pain or afraid, and the amount exceeds acceptable limits. The pain is warning him of danger. When you are tuned in to your baby, you can translate his behavior into a coherent message and feel confident in responding to it.

Expect to change your expectations

Rarely are parents prepared for the experience of caring for their first child. No one can fully anticipate how completely life changes. Your work load doubles, your sleep decreases, and what used to be downtime to sack out and relax has shrunk considerably. It's no easy task taking care of all the necessities of feeding, changing, playing with your baby and getting him to sleep, especially when you're tired. But out of all the challenges you face as a parent, one of the more difficult adjustments is getting comfortable with feeling out of control. You now have an unpredictable, on call, 24-hour-a-day, having-to-rise-to-the-occasion kind of job. At least with the housework you can decide when to get the laundry done or the dishes washed. If you're really too tired, or sick, your job can wait. Not so when taking care of a baby.

Imagine these scenarios: It's three in the morning and your little one won't go back to sleep. She's crying inconsolably, but you can't get her to settle down. Or, your two-year-old is climbing up on the table, reaching for your hot coffee. You gently put him down but within seconds he goes back again. Or, you're in the last aisle at the grocery store and your child has grabbed yet another forbidden item off the shelf. As you pry the item loose from her hands, she throws a tantrum. Such are the trials and tribulations of even the most well-intentioned parent.

When you are met with resistance from your child, your stress increases. Now you not only have to maneuver through the obstacle course of tears and yells, but you must struggle against your own tension as well. Because you are frustrated, keeping up with the tasks of dressing, feeding, and protecting your baby can become more important than how you get the job done. Instead of distracting your two-year-old with a new focus for his curiosity, you simply take the object of destruction out of his hands. Rather than humoring your baby while you get the strained peas out of his hair, you rush him through a bath and plunk him down into a wind-up swing. And if you have just endured a tumultuous session with your child, you may have few comforting words to offer, little awareness of what position you are holding him in, and may not make any eye contact whatsoever.

All of us have our bad days and have taken these short cuts with our children. But if we take too many of them, especially during infancy, a child's mental development and emotional well-being will suffer. Babies don't only need to be fed, changed and rocked. They need to feel that their physical sensations are manageable. They need to be unafraid and at ease in order to be available for learning. They need interaction, and for that they need to trust that their caretakers are consistently responsive to them. That's why it is so important that a parent's reactions are sympathetic. The more we can make our babies feel comfortable and secure, the sooner they can get on with the business of what they are also programmed to do: explore the world, test it out, master challenges, and prepare for independence. Emotional equilibrium allows babies to be available for these tasks rather than preoccupied with trying to cope with their upsets.

It would be nice, you might think, if your baby would just do exactly as you wish and not resist any of your good deeds. Wouldn't life be so much simpler if we could force our children to mind us and behave? (That probably isn't what you'd be thinking, however, if you were the child in question.) If we were to be honest, the plain truth would emerge that we want our children to obey us so they won't cause us grief. We want them to learn without trial and error, without making mistakes; to be patient so they don't interrupt us, and follow the directions that we know are good for them. When we've run out of patience, we want them to just stop. But it's not that simple. No amount of controlling your child will turn him into a person without needs.

The problem is, what children and parents require are different. Parents usually have too much to do, babies not enough. Parents like peace and quiet, babies like noise and excitement. Parents want cleanliness and order, babies want to throw, smear, rip, and turn over anything they can. The only similarity is that a parent wants his or her needs to be met first and so does a child. Children's needs, however, are more pressing than parents' needs because children are dependent on us and are still forming physically, emotionally and intellectually. Part of the package for you as a parent is to give more time, energy, and patience than you think you have. But the more parents can accept that their child is a person and deserves to be treated as such, the less they will be frustrated by trying to control their child. And the easier it will be to make the sacrifices parenting demands.

The spanking debate

Does this mean that we are at the beck and call of every one of our child's whims? Absolutely not. As your child comes into her own a little more (after 12 months of age), setting limits will be equally important to do. (See section on Spoiling) But even setting up limitations for a child requires time, energy and patience. It's quick and easy to hit and threaten children to make them behave, but a number of studies challenge this parenting practice, and the American Academy of Pediatrics recommends against it.

Recently published in the AMA's Archives of Pediatric and Adolescent Medicine is a study that came out of the University of New Hampshire and Texas Christian University on corporal punishment. Their findings show that common spankings (not abusive hitting) increased antisocial behavior in children. Children who were spanked as little as once a week lied, cheated, bullied others, and had more behavioral problems in school than children who weren't spanked. The more the child was spanked, the higher the level of antisocial behavior, regardless of race, gender or socioeconomic background. (This last finding confirms that the spanking was the cause of the resulting behavior as opposed to any other factor.)

This research only confirms what we have known since the first studies in behaviorism were done decades ago—children primarily learn through modeling or learning by example. For instance, toddlers acquire language and utilize complex rules of grammar without ever having been taught them. They accomplish this by observing the people around them speak.

Children imitate you constantly, every parent knows that. It shouldn't be surprising then to learn that spanking children teaches them by example to be aggressive—that it's acceptable to take advantage of or hurt others. When you spank your child you are modeling these values.

Even though we know that, as a mode of learning, modeling has the strongest influence on our children, it is not a very popular parenting strategy. Maybe that's because it means parents (and child experts) would have to be held accountable for *their* behavior as well.

When a child acts out, they might have to ask themselves, "How did I teach this child to act this way?" It is much easier to expound, "Do as I say, not as I do." It lets parents off the hook and they don't have to take responsibility for their less than perfect behavior. It feels better for parents to command from a position of power and authority and vent their frustration with a swat to their child's behind. It takes a real effort to regain one's composure and calmly teach a child right from wrong.

The word discipline originally comes from the Latin "disciplina" which means "to teach" and "to learn." Now it has come to mean "to punish." Your goal as a parent is to teach, not to punish. There are many effective ways to change your child's behavior other than hitting him—if you are willing to be in charge of your own behavior.

In order of effectiveness, modeled behavior has the most impact on children. The second most influential modifier is positive reinforcement, or the offering of rewards for positive behavior. Next, in order of influence is negative reinforcement, or the taking away of something desirable as a consequence. And the least effective behavior modifier is punishment, which too many people have been led to believe is the most powerful. (If that were true, we wouldn't have such a high rate of recidivism in our prison system.) Punishment seems effective because it makes the behavior stop for the period of time that the threat is present. But studies have shown that the long-term instructive value of punishment is almost nil. Once the parents are not around or are no longer a threat, the behavior is likely to return.

Our cultural bias in favor of using force and control over our children is taking its toll on us. We use spanking more than any other developed country and we are also the most violent western society. That one statistic alone should speak volumes to us. The problem begins with how we have been told to treat our infants.

In the past babies were shown who the boss was in a number of ways. They were put on eating schedules, toilet trained as soon as possible, spanked and left to cry themselves to sleep. Babies soon learned not to expect to get everything they wanted and to be independent before they were ready. Coddling to their need for play, stimulation, and comfort was thought to spoil them.

Instead, numerous studies have clearly shown:

- Babies who are left emotionally and physically hungry too often become needy and demanding children.

- Babies who aren't effective in getting their needs met will learn more extreme ways to manipulate and control their environment.

- Babies who are not consistently and sensitively responded to are rightfully angry about being left in their discomfort and have more tantrums as a result.

- These same babies are understandably anxious and have little tolerance for confrontation and delayed gratification.

- They feel bad and they are more desperate to have what they want when they want it. They are impatient and whiney.

- The so-called spoiled child is the one whose cries haven't been responded to and who learns to be extra loud and disruptive to get a caretaker's attention.

- The spoiled child hasn't had his or her species-specific needs met and has been exposed to unhealthy models of behavior.

On the other hand:

- Children who have been responded to and nurtured are much more likely to feel secure because their species-specific needs have been met.

- The baby who has been sensitively and consistently cared for is more likely to be respectful of others since that is how he or she has been treated.

- A baby who is consistently cared for learns to feel valued and therefore knows how to value the needs of others in return.

In other words the model of behavior that infants are exposed to shapes them more than any other form of behavior modification.

Childhood scars

If you have been taught to withhold from, regulate, be suspicious of, spank, or punish your child because this is how you were treated, it may be hard to believe another way is better. However, if you did have a difficult childhood, your own memories should confirm what you are reading here.

If your parents followed the controlling/withholding school of thought, or if they were dysfunctional themselves (depressed, addicted, or in some way unavailable), do you suffer from feelings of low self-worth and a low tolerance for stress? If you were shamed and yelled at for your mistakes, did it teach you or defeat you? If your parents hit you, did you learn your lesson or learn to fear your parents' wrath? Did it make you more thoughtful, or did it leave you angry and resentful? If you were told how bad you were, did it motivate you to be good or did you feel worthless? If you were abused, neglected, made to feel unsafe and insecure, do you find that you have a hard time trusting others? Do you often feel angry, anxious or depressed?.

As a psychotherapist I have heard many sad stories over the years and by far the saddest were the reports of childhood traumas. It wasn't just hearing about my clients' pain that was disturbing, it was the knowledge that at least some of it might have been avoided. If my clients' parents had just known what effect their words and their actions were having on their child, if they had known what the alternatives were, maybe their grown child wouldn't be discussing his depression with me today.

Parents can't take all the blame nor all the credit for how their children turn out, but they do have a powerful effect on them. They do the best job they know how to do. However, when they don't have the right information, or if they have been emotionally damaged themselves, it is difficult to do that job well.

Many people are stressed out these days, but parents are especially taxed. It's not easy dealing with all the demands with which they have to contend. What you learn here about bonding with your baby and supporting his or her emotional health will ultimately make your job easier, not harder. Information helps you make decisions and set goals. Being a responsive parent will help you to produce a child who is easier to live with.

However, this information should not be used as a stick with which to beat yourself up. If you were left with childhood scars, you are probably going to see your own pains and frustrations surface along with your child's. Sometimes you'll be able to be patient and loving; other times you won't. If you get down on yourself over all the times that you are not the perfect parent you will soon be unhappy and unable to enjoy your baby. Be patient and work on becoming a better parent a little each day.

It is normal at times to feel less than happy with life as a parent as long as that isn't what you feel most of the time. Babies require hard work; they limit your choices, and at times seem to be the source of your frustration. You'd have to be a saint not to grow tired of putting your needs on hold so much of the time. It's normal to have these feelings arise from time to time but staying in this state will bring misery to all. It is important then to let these upsets go and remind yourself that it's not your child's fault that she is dependent on you. You are doing a difficult and important job and it requires you to grow and develop along with your child. As parents we not only shape a life but are changed in the process. If we rise to the occasion we will find ourselves becoming more compassionate, patient and much more able to "roll with the punches" that life throws our way.

If we put ourselves in our children's shoes and imagine what it feels like to be comforted rather than screamed at, listened to rather than ignored, we can't go wrong. Parents who have a bond with their children are not likely to hurt or abuse them.

It's not easy to be caught in the middle of a change in traditional parenting philosophy. That's why you should make good use of the appendix in the back of this book. Get support from an organization, newsletter, or magazine. Go through the bibliography and review the research if it will help you to feel confident.

Don't expect others around you, including some professionals, to know about the recent studies that have come out in support of responsive parenting. Even though this information has been circulating for a number of years, it is only now beginning to trickle into the public mainstream.

There is a wonderful organization called *I Am Your Child,* founded by Rob Reiner and the Reiner Foundation. You may have seen a prime time special they produced that aired in 1997. Their mission is to educate the public about the importance of bonding, the need for responsive parenting and what babies need for optimal brain development. They have a free booklet and video available that outlines many of the basic principles found in this book. They can be reached at 1-888-447-3400.

What Babies Need

The devastating effects of maternal deprivation were observed by nuns and bishops, doctors, and foundling home workers for several hundred years, but were never correctly understood. Until very recently babies were considered to be little more than physiological lumps who surely did not possess the capacity to experience emotions. The idea that infants were capable of sadness, loneliness or depression was thought to be preposterous.

In fact it wasn't until the 1930s when men such as David Levy, a leader in the Child Guidance movement; Harold Skeels, from the Iowa Child Research Welfare Station; and Harry Bakwin, head of Bellevue Hospital's pediatric ward, wrote of their findings on maternal deprivation that this information received much attention. Even though it was well known that babies died at alarming rates in state and privately run institutions, the diagnosis was usually starvation, and the cause was written off to disease and genetic weaknesses. Even though in asylums, orphanages and hospitals, here and in Europe, infant mortality rates were as high as 75%, the connection between *emotional* malnutrition and a baby's failure to thrive was never made.

The worst-case scenarios came out of institutions that prided themselves on providing quality medical care and that took enormous precautions not to spread disease and germs around the wards. In the name of sterility and hygiene, babies were fed by propped up bottles and were almost never handled or touched. And yet their high rates of infant mortality were still thought to be from chronic infection rather than the lack of loving touch and a bond with a special someone.

Not until a British psychiatrist and researcher named John Bowlby came on the scene did maternal deprivation receive much attention from the psychoanalytic community. Based on his research on the infant-mother bond, Bowlby developed attachment theory. He and researcher Mary Ainsworth are credited with developing the first scientific studies on the subject in the 1950s and '60s. A number of subsequent studies have since replicated their findings and have further contributed to the reliability of attachment theory. Instead of guessing at and philosophizing about what a baby needs, as had been done in the past, they drew conclusions and formulated theories based on data collected in controlled laboratory settings. One of the more important studies, developed by Dr. Ainsworth, was called the Strange Situation. It is still in use today and is a primary tool for diagnosing attachment disorders—the result of infants' insecure bonds with their caretakers.

The Strange Situation study process begins with researchers observing, for several minutes, a mother and her twelve-month-old child together in a room that's unfamiliar to them. A stranger enters and first talks to the mother and then tries to engage the baby. Mother exits the room, leaving baby with the stranger. After a short time the mother returns. Then the stranger leaves and, after a few minutes, the mother leaves also. The baby is all alone. Soon the stranger returns and in few minutes more, the mother does also. During these interactions babies are not prompted by their mothers to behave in specific ways.

Before the lab experiments where the Strange Situation was introduced, Dr. Ainsworth conducted lengthy interviews with the mothers and observed the mother and child in their home. A baseline of what was "normal" or usual behavior for that child was established, which allowed for temperament to be seen as an individual characteristic apart from a pattern of insecure attachment. Based on the information the mothers offered and their early observations, the researchers found they could predict which children would be diagnosed with attachment disorders. This established a firm connection between the attitudes and actions of the mother as the causal factor in predicting the child's response when faced with an unusually insecure situation.

This predictive power of relating the cause—the mother's attitude and behavior—to the effect—the signs of attachment disorder—lent that much more credibility to the results. In addition, the studies were important because they examined the relationship between mother and child rather than assessing them as individuals. The characteristics of the babies' behaviors were not considered as important as how they acted in relation to others and their environment. Furthermore, the experiments have since been repeated numerous times and evaluated in blind studies to preserve accuracy. Scientists independently arrived at similar conclusions in their assessments.

The results that are repeatedly demonstrated by the Strange Situation are that consistently unresponsive, inconsistent and/or insensitive childcare will almost always result in behaviors and feelings in a baby that are dysfunctional and undesirable. But who determines how a healthy baby is supposed to act? What is the standard? Nature sets the standard. Behaviors and feelings that hinder or disrupt a baby's natural development and disturb his or her ability to productively interact with the world are labeled as unhealthy.

From the Strange Situation studies and others like them we can begin to understand what a baby's security needs are and what we need to do as parents to help.

So what does a baby need to be emotionally, intellectually, and socially healthy?

He or she needs:

- To feel loved
- To feel safe (which primarily means proximity to a trusted caretaker)
- To be physically comfortable
- To be stimulated by interacting with you and the world
- To be sensitively and consistently responded to

The baby's job is to mature, which means he or she needs to have enough security and focus, enough emotional equilibrium in order to learn and explore. To be successful in life, babies need to be attentive and tuned in, learn to discriminate between safe and not safe, trust themselves, feel confident in their own abilities, learn how to give and take and cooperate with others. They need emotions that can go from being upset back to a place of equilibrium, and they need the energy, enthusiasm, and the absence of distracting upsets to accomplish the ultimate goal—that of developing autonomy.

The findings from the Strange Situation established categories and groups of behaviors that are found in insecurely and securely attached children. Even though there are a variety of ways insecurely attached children act, there are some behaviors that distinguish them from securely attached children. In general, they are handicapped in their ability to use mom as a secure base, to explore and interact with their environment, and to recover from upsets.

The following are descriptions of the major categories of attachment as defined by the first Strange Situation studies (researchers have since added more sub-categories):

Secure attachment—One-year-olds will feel safe enough to explore a new environment while mother is present, and will usually, although not always, be somewhat upset when she leaves. If these babies do get upset however, their distress is manageable. The secure child is naturally wary of strangers, finds them tolerable if mother is present, but would not want to be comforted by them if she were not. Upon mother's return, a securely attached baby will be happy to see her, and will melt into the comfort of her arms. Once comforted, the baby will continue to explore the environment, periodically looking back at the mother for a reassuring glance.

The mothers in this category are warm and loving toward their babies and consistently and sensitively respond to them most of the time.

Ambivalent attachment—Babies in this category will be demanding and clingy with the mother, and not put at ease by her presence. Rather than explore the environment they stay by her side. When mother leaves they become extremely upset, even angry, especially when the stranger is in the room. Upon mother's return these babies will typically act in one of two ways. Either they will passively sit in distress, unable to clearly signal or receive the mother's comfort, or they will initially seek the mother's comfort but then resist her. They may even strike out at her, or throw a tantrum. They seem to be saying, "I feel abandoned too much by you. I'm angry and confused. I'm not sure I should risk getting close to you." The mistrust these babies feel for their mothers interferes with their ability to recover from upsets and to explore the environment. They don't trust anyone else to be in control and they don't accept limit setting very well.

The mothers in these cases are often inconsistent, unpredictable and insensitive in how they respond to their babies. Their responses are often out of sync with their babies' needs.

Avoidant attachment—These babies appear to be very independent and self-contained, but a closer examination reveals some disturbing patterns. They may explore their environment but do so without showing much interest in what they find. They may pick up a toy but will not be curious to see how it works. These babies show little concern when the mother leaves and upon her return don't move to greet her. Instead they either ignore or intentionally avoid her. When picked up they will arch their backs, stiffen, or push away from the mother and avoid eye contact. They don't trust her affection and defend themselves from the possibility of further rejection by avoiding or rejecting her.

Unlike most babies, these children are willing to go off with strangers, especially if they think the stranger might give them something they want (such as food, entertainment, etc.) These babies can be deceptively charming and affectionate, but they act this way in order to have more control over unreliable caretakers and uncertain future events.

On the surface they seem unaffected by the mother's absence and the presence of a stranger, but all the more reason to be concerned. This is not a sign of self-confidence. Their behavior seems to be saying, "Because no one has consistently and sensitively cared for me, I don't know how to care about others and trust them."

Serious emotional problems are likely to develop later on in life if this disorder is left untreated.

The mothers in this category are very inconsistent in their care and sometimes are disturbed themselves. They may suffer from depression or other disorders. They offer little eye contact and are not tuned into their infants' needs.

In the original studies all the babies were cared for at home and not left in daycare. The experience of abandonment or rejection occurred because the mother was ineffective, emotionally off balance, or preoccupied with herself, the cause being perhaps depression, immaturity, or stressful life circumstances. In current studies, "abandonment" can also be found when the mother or father is absent for too many hours a week, substitute care is inadequate, a parent dies or leaves, the child or parent has to undergo a lengthy hospitalization or separation, or if the child experiences chronic pain.

These categories of attachment behaviors are guidelines that help to define the problems of the insecurely attached child. Only an experienced professional in the field should assess a child for possible Reactive Attachment Disorders (RAD), the consequence of a history of insufficient care. The DSM-IV, the diagnostic manual of psychological disorders, defines RAD as inappropriate social behavior that occurs before a child is five years old. The child manifests extremely indifferent and contrary responses and/or indiscriminate attachments. Additional features include aggressiveness, poor impulse control and developmental lags.

The following is a more complete list of the signs of an insecure attachment in babies or small children. They:

- Avoid making eye contact (on parent's terms)

- Are rigid when you try to hold and cuddle them, or

- Limp and don't respond to cuddling (on parent's terms)

- Are inappropriately demanding or clingy, or the opposite is true,

- Would just as easily go off with a stranger as with a parent

- Are withdrawn and too quiet, or

- Full of rage and tend to engage in tantrums

- Hoard or gorge food

- Frequently attempt to control their parent's behavior with tantrums, displays of affection, etc.

- Have problems with impulse control

- Lag in development (not to be confused with normal variations in reaching the milestones of crawling, walking, talking, etc.)

There are other reasons why a child may be acting in this way, but a lack of a secure attachment is a good possibility.

When a baby is first born he has so many new experiences to adjust to and sensations to get used to. Many of his systems are still developing. For instance, his respiration is irregular, his nervous system is immature, and vision and motor responses are still uncoordinated. Your first task as a parent is to help your newborn make a smooth transition into the world. You can do this by creating for your baby the same kind of environment he had inside the womb (more on this in the chapters immediately following). By continuing to provide many of the same sensations your baby had in utero you provide him with the opportunity to slowly settle in and adjust to his new surroundings. This means that baby's systems for coping won't be overtaxed and more harmonious states can become the norm.

How long this transition takes depends on the infant. Normally the initial organization period takes around three months. High need, overly sensitive, premature, adopted, previously hospitalized, colicky babies, or babies in a lot of pain often need an extended period of special handling, perhaps as long as 9 to 12 months. You will know when your baby has matured out of the newborn stage because he will have longer and more restful sleeping patterns, will be eating well, will be easily soothed and will be able to start interacting with his environment.

By six months of age your infant will start wanting more exchanges with the outside world, and more play time, but he will still want to be close to you. His need for you as his secure base will gradually taper off, but over the course of years, not months.

Between 6 to 12 months a baby's feelings of secure or insecure attachment will be more visible. Leaving you may become very disturbing. When children go through stages of increasing autonomy, their need for security can also increase. This is normal. However, if a baby often sits dazed or uninterested, anxious or fretful about exploring his environment, or if he is frantic every time you walk away, he is exhibiting a need for more security. This usually means more proximity to a trusted caretaker.

The amount of time your baby wants and needs to be close to his parents goes hand in hand with how much he depends on them to keep him alive and well. By the time he is three and is feeding himself, going without diapers, and getting down his own toys, your role will have gradually changed from total provider to part-time provider. Now the newborn who you carried and nursed almost continuously has become a slightly more independent child and therefore your bonding strategies will shift. You will still be listening to his needs and responding to his fears, you will still need to be a safe base for him to return to, but you will also need to allow for more exploration and attempts at independence.

The next five chapters will explore in depth the best ways to form and maintain a bond between you and your baby. They are to:

- Get support for yourself
- Learn to tune in and read your baby's needs
- Breastfeed
- Hold and carry your baby often
- Provide for his or her nighttime security

Support

In order to tune in to your baby it is important that you tune into yourself. The less stressed out you are the less stressed your baby will be. Babies are like little sponges. They soak up all the sights, sounds and feelings around them. You may be able to keep up a frantic pace and hold it together, but your baby won't be able to and he'll tell you loud and clear. And, your child's distress will only add to yours.

You've just entered into a whole new life and it is natural to feel overwhelmed. Going through the pregnancy and birth alone can be a roller coaster of emotions and sensations for both parents. You experience fear and anticipation before the birth, pain and exhaustion while giving birth, followed by elation afterwards when you first hold your infant in your arms. Then after the birth come the sleepless nights, the shock of how much work is involved, the feelings of joy from sharing this occasion with friends and family, and the indescribable "holy cow, I'm a parent" moment. It's a lot to deal with in a short amount of time.

You and your baby need time to recuperate. For the first few weeks it's a good idea to keep things as simple as you can. Limit visitors, sleep whenever your baby sleeps, and try to get help with meals and laundry. You want your focus to be on your baby so he can feel loved and secure and you can begin to bond with each other.

All new parents need assistance. The phrase "it takes a village to raise a child" is more true than you might imagine. Hillary Rodham Clinton's book, *It Takes a Village*, perfectly describes the importance of family and community support in the raising of healthy children. We are not meant to handle this enormous task of raising a child by ourselves. Our family structures were originally set up to exist within tribes. Families today, even those containing two parents, are hard pressed to manage on their own. Single parents perform nothing less than heroic acts on a daily basis. Extended families are a thing of the past and good affordable childcare is equally hard to find. That's the bad news.

The good news is that you can find the help you need if you look for it. These are very difficult times for parents because support is not around in abundance, but it is around. You will have to seek it out and learn to ask for what you need.

Slowly but surely, employers are supporting parents by providing longer leave time and on-site childcare, but many times you will have to ask for them. There are grassroots movements in the works to revitalize neighborhoods and rekindle community, but you might need to be the organizer in your area. In small but significant ways parents are banding together and supporting each other, because it is painfully obvious parents can't do it alone and have sane lives. Find those people in your neighborhood or your town who share your predicament. There are people in your community who have the time, information or expertise who can help you. The trick is to reach out and ask for support.

The first obstacle you have to get over is being afraid to ask for help. Many of us are hesitant to reach out because we are shy or we don't want to be perceived of as weak. The plain fact is that we do not and can not live without depending on each other. You don't feel shy about buying the food you need, but you depend on someone else to produce it. When you pay money for a product or service, it's an equal exchange. You don't owe anybody anything and it feels okay. But there are other ways besides money to get what you need. If you ask a favor from a neighbor, offer to cook a meal in return (while you cook your own). If you need childcare, work out trades with other mothers you trust. The worst that can happen is that the other person will say no.

If money, time, skills, or physical or emotional health keep you from taking good care of your child, then find the people or person who can help you. Right now, taking good care of your baby is too important to let shyness or pride control you. If you are isolated and experiencing a lot of stress, you are going to have a harder time bonding with your baby.

If it is difficult for you to ask for help, then practice becoming more assertive. Talk into a mirror and get used to the feeling of asking for what you want. Pretend to make a request, then answer yourself back with all the responses you fear you might hear in real life. Typically, most people discover that they are afraid of rejection or don't want others to think they're needy or weak. Or maybe you'll find that you're afraid of being in a sharing relationship with someone and are worried that too much will be asked of you in return. These are the main reasons people don't ask for help but you should explore what your reasons are. When you think you've rehearsed enough, start out slowly by asking a family member or good friend for a minor favor such as picking up something for you at the store. Then work your way up to more difficult requests.

You may discover that some of the blocks you have, in asking for what you want, run deep and, admittedly, are hard to change. You don't transform low self-esteem into self-confidence overnight. However, you can still learn to act with self-confidence even if you don't feel self-confident. Acting as if you are assertive, as if you are worthwhile, will help you get your needs met, even though you may be uncomfortable asking. By practicing in a mirror, or in your head, you will get used to being assertive and, as a result, you'll feel a little more in control.

Having children touches on so many areas of one's life: health, finances, marital and family relationships, jobs, time, sleep, energy—you are going to experience some upheaval. You may find issues surfacing now that you have been keeping on hold, or have tucked away where you never think about them. Resentments you've been holding onto or concerns about your job or career may bubble up. The question of how long to stay at home can bring up fears of becoming isolated, or financially strapped. The change in routines and sleep patterns alone will cause unrest.

For some people these changes will be harder to cope with than for others, and often the difference depends on how much support is available. Support can make the difference between experiencing tolerable levels of stress or the kind that is off the Richter scale. Getting the help you need is part of being a responsible parent, whether your source is family, friends, and neighbors, or the professional help of doctors, counselors and clergy.

A list of sources for support:

La Leche League—This a wonderful organization and very dedicated to assisting new families. They specialize in help with breastfeeding but they also know about other resources in your town. Their national number is 1-800-LA LECHE.

Birth Preparation Class Members—If you took a birth preparation class, contact some of the people in your group. They will share many of the same concerns you have. You can exchange information, shop for each other, and in general feel the support of people who are going through what you are. You may be able to work out babysitting trades allowing you to work part-time, without having to pay for childcare. Later you can also organize a play group for the babies.

Form a "New Moms Group"—The purpose of the group could be anything you want. It could be purely social or a place to exchange ideas and share concerns. Or you might want to set up childcare trades either with one mom or in teams where two mothers babysit together while the other two moms are gone. Company is often a welcome change to the sometimes lonely routine of caring for a baby.

To get it started, put up flyers announcing the formation of a group for new moms. Post them at baby stores, doctor's offices, and with midwives. Your role is to act as contact person and to set up the first meeting, not necessarily to be the leader. Good places to meet could be a room in a church or at a park.

Midwives—Call your hospital if you have trouble finding a listing in the phone book. They will be able to help you connect with other new moms. They may also have information about nutrition and postpartum depression.

County Mental Health—usually a counseling resource in every town. If finances are a problem, these agencies have sliding scales. A counselor can be someone who answers questions, reassures you, helps you work on problems in your relationships, or helps you find the cause of your depression or anxiety. You don't have to think you're "abnormal" to want to see a counselor.

Your Local Hospital—Ask for the social services department. The hospital may sponsor classes or support groups for new moms and dads.

Spiritual Organizations—If you belong to a church or temple, find out if there are resources for you there. If you don't belong to a spiritual organization maybe now is the time to join one. You may find a community for yourself and a source of comfort.

The Library—Take out books about raising children. The more you know the better you'll feel and the more prepared you will be when new situations come up. The library also will have a list of community resources. Ask the librarian for help.

Have a Friend Over—such as another new mom, even if you don't know each other that well. You're both in the same situation and just talking over your frustrations and concerns can make you feel better. Or have some fun together. Play board games or cards. Cook some meals or do laundry together. Having company can make the work less boring.

Support Yourself—You will inevitably go through periods of self-doubt about your abilities as a parent; this is common. It shows you are concerned. Don't criticize yourself. If you aren't living up to your expectations then change your expectations. Criticizing yourself will leave you feeling defeated. If you want to improve yourself then use a method that works. The best way to make a life change is by forming very short-term goals that are attainable. If you want to lose weight, for example, then pick a very small goal to reach. "Today I won't drink soda and I'll exercise for 10 minutes." This you can do successfully. When you feel successful, you'll want to do more.

In terms of parenting, your priority is to engage in as many nurturing and bonding activities as possible. Start by adding one behavior at a time. "Today I will give my baby reassuring eye contact when I pick him up." The next week add more skin to skin contact. Set goals for successful breastfeeding or focus on obtaining adequate childcare. Work on the interventions that will be the most meaningful.

It doesn't help to make blanket statements such as, "I'm so ugly. I'm such a loser. I'm such a terrible parent." These statements are never true. Everyone has something unique and good about them. Focus on the positive.

You need to take care of yourself so you will have what it takes to be a responsive parent. Create ways of renewing yourself that fit into family life. You will be going out less than you used to, but you can still have satisfying experiences at home. Make a list of activities that renew you and which are family friendly, and put them into these categories: **physical, intellectual, emotional,** and **spiritual.** Parents often need a lot of rest and relaxation, so under physical you might have: getting a massage from your mate, taking a hot bath, or all taking a walk together before dinner. Intellectual stimulation can also be a stress reducer. Under this category you could list: listening to a book on tape (you can usually rent them from the library or a video store) while playing with your baby, or playing scrabble with your mate instead of watching TV in the evening. Emotional support could include: talking (even complaining) to a good friend, starting a journal, beating a pillow to vent your frustration, or setting aside a "do something special for yourself" day. Spiritual support may be something as simple as listening to inspiring music, singing to your baby (yes, singing—it can be very uplifting), going to a spiritual service once a week, being in nature, or sitting quietly in the sun. Put this list up where you will see it often. When you're feeling out of sorts or stressed out, tune into what area(s) could use your attention.

If you're a single mom it is vital that you get all the support you can. You might even think about shared living arrangements with another single parent. You can share childcare, cut down on expenses, and, in general, feel less isolated.

Know that there is help out there and that you and your baby deserve to be supported.

Tuning In

What babies think and feel may seem like a complete mystery at times. They can't tell you what they want or point to where it hurts. They can't even tell you, "Nothing is wrong, I just feel like crying." When you try to understand your infant's communication it will be like playing a game of charades, as you guess at the meaning of a fuss or a cry. But an answer will almost always be revealed if you tune into your baby. You will be able to decipher the signs and learn what is normal for your particular child. Questions like "Should my infant be staring off this much, awake so little, wanting to be held so often?" are ones you will be able to answer with confidence (and, if you are in doubt, consult a professional).

If your baby is crying and you can't figure out what's wrong you may find yourself pleading, "Just tell me what you want." But that is precisely what she is doing. If she cries when you put her down, she is saying, "I feel too insecure to be away from you." If she smiles when you talk to her, she is saying, "I enjoy interacting with you." If she seems fretful, your baby may be trying to tell you, "I feel awful. Just hold me while I cry." Babies who are inconsolable in the late afternoon no matter what techniques you use for calming, sometimes just need to let off steam. But they will still need to be comforted.

When your baby puts out a message, it's like the question to a riddle. When you answer correctly, you help the pieces of the puzzle fit together. You give meaning to the confusion. For infants everything is new and they need help putting their scattered experiences in order. When you are tuned in and respond correctly to one of your baby's attempts to communicate, you are helping to organize her world. Your in-sync response helps your baby figure out how desire and sensation fit together. When a caretaker answers her cues, the baby learns which feelings go with which responses and what to expect next time. The coupling of sensation with event creates the model baby draws from and uses as the representation of herself in the world. Through the repetition of experience baby learns what works, what doesn't and adjusts her behavior accordingly. She adapts to the pattern she's exposed to (even if it's neglect).

In their first few months infants move in and out of various states, from fully asleep to fully awake. Approximately every four hours they will either be winding up to eat, play, fuss or cry, or winding back down to slumber. If you carefully observe your baby, you will notice her move through these states. You can help your baby feel in harmony with her environment by matching your activity with her condition. When your baby just wakes up and starts to fuss, ease her into being sufficiently awake before you try to play peek-a-boo or make attempts to cheer her up. During the periods when your infant is bright-eyed and alert, talk, sing or play with her—don't put her in a crib, isolated from stimulation. If your baby is awake and hungry, help her to focus on nursing. If you talk to her too much she will be distracted by the sound of your voice and will stop feeding.

Tune into whether or not your baby is calmly able to focus on you or is preoccupied with feeling uncomfortable. Conversations with your infant occur when she is in a state referred to as quiet alertness. You can tell by looking at her that she is available for interaction. This is when your baby is most available for learning about the world and playing with you.

When you want to have eye contact while conversing with your baby, set her at an angle in front of your face. When you look at each other, you may notice that a kind of dialogue naturally develops. It begins with you looking at the baby, while she is gazing back at you. Then you smile and she smiles back. Next she initiates the conversation and coos, excitedly moving her arms and legs, and you say something cooing back—it's a game of follow the leader. You let your baby be the leader and then you add something new to the conversation—offer a finger to grasp or put her hand on your cheek and let her feel your face. Respond to her touch with delight. Or you might hold her feet and ask, "Are these your little feet?" When she squeals her reply, you smile with appreciation, affirming her correct answer. This dialogue tells your baby, "I recognize your abilities," and "I understand what you are trying to tell me."

During your conversations, watch your baby go through a cycle of tuning into your face, responding to your voice and then turning her attention away. You'll see her reaching out into the world, getting stimulated, and then tuning out again in order to recover. Babies can take in just so much at one time. When you notice your baby turn away, let her disengage. She needs that break from stimulation.

Monitor how much stimulation your infant can take and modify your behavior to match your baby's ability to handle that excitement level. Your job is to recognize when you've gotten too far ahead, or too far behind your baby's lead. If play gets to be too stimulating, tone down your excitement and show baby how to calm down. Offer gentle rocking and soothing words in order to demonstrate to your infant solutions for distress. After a few moments baby will either return for more play or she will transition into a different state. This means: end of conversation and on to more pressing needs.

Some babies may be distracted and will need to be gently wooed into making eye contact and joining into a conversation. They need a more focused and gentler kind of treatment and require you to spend more time helping them feel comfortable. Pre-term and adopted children can take longer to make the transition, as can colicky babies. These infants will often be agitated and fretful, or at the other end of the spectrum, passive and unresponsive. They are ineffective communicators and need you to help them engage in a dialogue. When your baby is always fussing or never tuned in, it is easy to feel discouraged. But high-need babies, especially, need your fine tuning and persistence to help them to settle in and feel connected. **This category of infants tends to form a group at higher risk for attachment disorders.**

After a short time you will get to know what kind of individual your baby is. You'll learn what kind of voice she responds to (most seem to prefer a kind of slow, sing-songy voice called Parentese), and what kind of play she prefers—soft and gentle or tickling and bouncing. You will discover whether she sleeps better in a quiet room or a noisy one. You'll notice a pattern of fussy times of the day, and the best way to hold her when she's upset.

Soon you'll be able to distinguish between your baby's four types of cries that translate into **hunger, pain, discomfort,** or **boredom.**

Sometimes the message you get from your baby is vague and you're not sure what's going on. You have to rely on your intuition to tell you what to do. Many people think there is no such thing as mother's intuition or at best, that it's too imprecise to be useful. You'd be surprised how clear and accurate that inner voice can be. The trick is to believe in your hunches. The more you believe in your sensing abilities the louder those signals will become. Mothers have a distinct advantage in this area, but dads or significant caregivers who spend a lot of time with your child will have these intuitions as well.

To help you begin to pinpoint what could be wrong with your fussy child, here is a list of some of the more common discomforts.

Physically Uncomfortable

- Hungry or thirsty
- Needs burping
- Has gas (try gently massaging tummy in circular clockwise motion)
- Sick (feels warm, is pale, agitated, not eating, etc.)
- Is too hot, which is more likely than too cold
- Wants to be bundled or swaddled (if he or she is a newborn)
- Needs to change positions
- Is allergic or sensitive to synthetic materials, perfumes, smoke or strong odors

- Needs low lights and low sounds
- Diaper needs changing
- Diaper rash
- Teeth coming in (usually drooling, sucking, and gumming a lot)
- Digestion problems
- Hurt him or herself
- Put something bad tasting in his or her mouth
- Undiagnosed medical problem (if you suspect this, see a doctor)

Emotionally Upset

- Afraid because he or she isn't being held
- Afraid because she or he is alone
- Afraid because there is yelling or loud noises
- Startled by a sudden movement
- Afraid of an unfamiliar sensation
- Upset by being held by unfamiliar people (visible by 6 to 9 months but exists for younger babies as well)
- Upset because the primary caretaker isn't making eye contact enough and/or is displaying a flat, emotionless face

Mentally Frustrated

- Bored, not enough visual stimulation (especially infants)
- Bored, not enough sensations

- Bored, not enough play
- Too much stimulation
- Not allowed to be in charge of interactions, *i.e.* when to turn away or change level of excitement
- Not assisted in exploring environment

A good all-around remedy for a distressed baby is infant massage. Besides relaxing babies it teaches them about how to let go and release their physical tension. Babies can start tuning into how they hold certain muscles and how they can control their discomfort by relaxing their bodies. In addition, massage stimulates their circulation, digestion, organ function, and the elimination of toxins, not to mention stimulating the brain. Many hospitals routinely use infant massage on premature or sick babies and find it greatly improves their recovery. I encourage you to find a book on the subject. A couple of titles are mentioned in the appendix.

You may not always be able to soothe your baby, but she will still feel more secure with your attention than without it. Just talking to your baby and reassuring her can be all she needs to get through a crisis. However, if you ever feel uneasy about how your baby is acting and your worry persists, don't hesitate to get help.

Breastfeeding

One of the very best things you can do for your infant is to breastfeed. Even if you have started and stopped, have gone back to work, had a cesarean section, have a premature baby, or even if you have adopted a child (it's true; more on this later), you can still breastfeed. There are so many advantages on every level—physically, emotionally and intellectually—it is difficult to exaggerate just how invaluable breastfeeding is. Even part-time nursing is better than no time at all.

Breast milk is what nature intended a baby's first food to be. To date, no formula or substitute comes anywhere near to imitating it. Scientists are just beginning to identify the hundreds of breast milk chemicals. It isn't surprising, though, how complex a substance breast milk is when one considers the important role it plays.

Breastfeeding is one of the key evolutionary strategies designed to not just keep babies alive but provide for what they need to grow and thrive. In all mammals, the mother's milk is designed to help their young meet whatever they will be specifically challenged by. Baby walruses get very fatty milk because fat is what they need to survive. In our species the most uniquely important task is to become thinking beings. Growing a healthy brain is our most important task (which includes having properly functioning endocrine and nervous systems to name but a few of the functions affected). Breast milk has been designed to meet all those challenges. Formula has not.

Obstacles to Successful Breastfeeding

In recent history, the bottle has won favor over the breast. It would be difficult to identify all the factors responsible for turning the tide, but it may be that the trend started with the moral attitudes that evolved during the Victorian era. Repression of one's sexuality and anything that remotely suggested sensuality became a commandment of the highest order. Breastfeeding began to be viewed as suggestive, immodest, even an unseemly act. Because mothers felt they had to be at home to nurse, interaction with the outside world was greatly curtailed. When women started moving into the workplace, because of war, poverty, or liberation, they found nursing to be confining. When commercial formula and bottles started being widely advertised, women were further encouraged to give up on breastfeeding.

All of these influences are alive and well today and still stand in the way of some women's decision to nurse. Maybe they are uncertain if it's appropriate to breastfeed in public (it is). They may not think they can nurse if they go back to work (they can), and formula manufacturers do what they can to lure mothers into buying their products. However, we can no longer ignore the numerous scientific studies that expound on the significance of breastfeeding.

We can't let outdated cultural beliefs stand in the way of doing what is best for our babies. It is very unfortunate that women have been made to feel embarrassed or shy about breastfeeding.

We are so conditioned to seeing the breast as a sexual object, some women may find it difficult to think of their breasts as the source of baby's nourishment instead of an object of sensual pleasure. They may worry that nursing in public will appear sexual. But if anything, seeing a nursing mother usually evokes a universal response of tenderness. Sure, there are always a few people who are going to be embarrassed by it. But breastfeeding is a natural and important act.

If you have to go back to work, you can still give your baby breast milk most of the time. (Call La Leche League for more in-depth information on working out the details.) There are a lot of different ways to do it. Breast milk can be pumped ahead of time and stored; babies can be brought to the work place or visited at lunch time or given formula during the day and nursed at night. On the weekends you would want to try to nurse exclusively in order to keep your supply of milk up. Your supply depends on the baby's demand for it.

Don't be concerned about leaking breasts (which is only an issue for a short time and can be controlled with pads) or that you are going to be more exhausted from nursing. Stress is also exhausting—much more so than breastfeeding. One of the perks for a nursing mom is that tranquilizing chemicals are released in her body that are calming to baby as well as to herself. Breastfeeding moms, like all moms, may feel tired if they don't eat nutritious foods, drink lots of fluids and get plenty of rest, but nursing doesn't have to overtax you.

Another concern women have is that they won't have enough milk. This is almost never the case. (By the way, small breasts have nothing to do with how much milk can be produced.) Mothers often don't realize that it takes up to five to seven days after the birth for the real milk to come in. Initially just a small amount of milk called colostrum is produced, but it is very rich. It is chock full of important infection-fighting substances and other regulating chemicals, and contains *all* that a baby needs.

A worry for some mothers is the frequency with which newborns nurse. Sometimes it's every twenty minutes over a three-hour period. This phase passes quickly though, and soon baby's little tummy can start holding more at a single feeding. There will be other times however, during growth spurts, when your baby will again nurse often, but this period won't last long either. When you are in one of those phases, enjoy the closeness and trust you are building with your infant. As your baby gazes up at you, take in the magic of this very special bond. Before you know it your baby will be squirming away to explore her new found freedom and you will never again have quite the same closeness as you did during those sweet moments of breastfeeding.

It is important not to hurry baby's nursing session. Let him tell you when he's done. The milk that babies receive when they begin eating will be less fatty than what they receive after they've been sucking for a while. If you rush them they won't get that important fattier milk. However, sometimes babies won't want to have a big meal. They will just want a few sips or some emotional comfort. Soon you'll know the difference between mealtime and snack time, or cuddling time, and you will feel comfortable with your baby's routine. A common pattern is to nurse on one side for a few minutes, burp baby, then change sides. After a few minutes, burp baby and nurse again on the side you started with. If you have a baby that tends to be sleepier, this switching will help keep him interested in nursing until he is full. However, if your baby never gets back to the first breast to get the fattier milk, stick with one breast per meal.

Tips for Successful Breastfeeding

There are a few tips that you should know to have a successful and enjoyable experience with breastfeeding. The best things to do are to read a book, take a class, or consult with a lactation specialist to get a full understanding of all the ins and outs, but the following pointers will get you started.

Two of the most important guidelines for successful breastfeeding are to make sure your baby, (1) has latched on properly and, (2) is positioned correctly. There are a number of ways to hold your baby, but, in short, you want baby's mouth to be facing the nipple and not pulling up, down or sideways on it. If you are cradling baby in front of you, think about holding the baby so that his tummy is facing your tummy. Have your baby's face close to your breast so he isn't pulling on your nipple in order to suck. You may fear your baby will suffocate if he's pulled in too close. Just push in slightly on the area of your breast that's right above his nose if your breast is covering his nostril and keeping him from breathing comfortably. (Babies can breathe through their mouths while nursing but some need or prefer nose breathing.) If you've had a cesarean section, try positioning the baby so that his body is straddled next to your side and his mouth is face on to your breast. This position, called the football hold, will keep your baby from pressing on your sutures.

To make sure your infant latches on properly, tickle his cheek closest to your breast or rub your nipple over his mouth. This will make him start "rooting" or looking to latch on to your breast. As soon as he opens his mouth wide, pull him close and put your whole nipple area into his mouth. You may need to pull down slightly on your baby's chin to make sure his mouth is open wide enough. Your baby needs to suck on the brownish area around your nipple, the areola, in order to properly activate the release of your milk. If baby only sucks on your nipple, or if he pulls down on it while sucking, you are going to get very sore very quickly. Other than a short, beginning period of toughening up your nipples, breastfeeding should not hurt. If it does, your baby probably hasn't latched on properly. When feeding is done, make sure you break your baby's suction by putting your finger in his mouth before pulling him off your breast—a nipple can be pulled just so far before it hurts.

If you start getting hard and very full breasts that are tender to the touch, it may mean you are becoming *engorged.* This condition is usually the result of a baby latching on improperly. The baby is sucking on the nipple, which is stimulating milk production, but because he isn't sucking on the areola, the milk isn't being released. To alleviate this problem alternate cool packs on your breasts between feedings. Then, right before you nurse, take a warm shower or apply a warm pack to your breasts and pump out some of your milk to relieve a little bit of the pressure. Again, make sure baby has latched on properly and feed him frequently as opposed to letting your baby linger at your breast for longer periods of nursing.

Make sure your nipples air dry before you re-dress. Let the milk dry naturally on your nipples rather than wiping it off. Breast milk will keep your nipples from cracking. Avoid using soap on your nipples; it will dry them out. But if your breasts do start cracking, apply Lansinoh, a pure lanolin product. Avoid oils or creams; they can aggravate the problem.

In general you want to be as relaxed as you can when you nurse. A tense mother will make it difficult and unpleasant for baby to nurse and this will upset the natural routine of breastfeeding. Spend several minutes relaxing before you get started. This makes it easier for your milk to let down. Lying in bed is a good position and may encourage you to nap with your baby. Or find a quiet corner where the two of you can be alone. Put pillows under your arm or on your tummy, and one under your supporting arm. Bring baby up to your level; don't hunch over to nurse. Rockers are ideal, but any comfortable chair with arm supports will do. Also make sure baby isn't too bundled up and don't wear perfume, lotion or anything else unpleasant tasting or strong smelling on or near your breasts. And watch what you eat. Whatever you put in your mouth is received by your baby. Certain foods and medications can upset your baby's stomach, or even be a danger to him.

Some women don't want to breastfeed because they don't want to restrict or monitor what they eat and drink. It is an understandable feeling. I dearly missed eating spicy food when I was breastfeeding. But nursing is so incredibly beneficial for you and your baby, the sacrifices you may make are really so minor in comparison. Ultimately what you both gain is much greater than what you give up.

La Leche League (1-800-LA LECHE) is your best source of breastfeeding help, but if for some reason there isn't a branch in your area call your doctor, the hospital, or a midwife to help you find the support you need. Like parenting, breastfeeding may require that you adjust to certain routines and maybe some strange feelings. At first you may think you could never get used to using an electric breast pump, or the routine of storing and transporting breast milk, or whatever your particular situation requires. But give yourself a real chance at adjusting. As has been said many times in this book, adaptation is what we do best, and what seems uncomfortable today can become old hat in a month's time.

Benefits of Breastfeeding

Here are eighteen reasons why you should consider breast-feeding your baby:

1. While you nurse, chemicals are released which have a tranquilizing effect. Not only do these chemicals help to calm you but they relax your baby, too.

2. These chemicals also boost your inclination to nurture and amplify your mother's intuition, helping you to get in tune with your baby.

3. There are 400 brain-building chemicals in breast milk that are not found in formula, cow's milk, goat's milk or anything else you could try as a substitute. The brain is the most important organ for a human being's survival. Nature has provided nutrients in breast milk to make sure the brain develops properly.

4. Studies have shown that breastfed babies have higher IQ's than bottlefed babies.

5. The proteins in breast milk are specifically made so that babies can easily digest them. They provide very specific growth-producing elements not found in formulas. These proteins also help to maintain a very important balance of just the right bacteria in the lining of the intestines.

6. The fats in breast milk are uniquely formulated to be utilized by human babies. These fats contribute to nerve production in the brain and provide certain hormones and vitamins. Formula is essentially absent of anything similar.

7. Breast milk helps protect your baby's health because it contains natural antibiotics and millions of white blood cells that fight off illnesses. The less your baby is sick, the less you will be spending on doctors, taking time off from work, and up in the middle of the night.

8. A substance called progesterone, which helps to regulate breathing, is found at higher levels in breastfed babies.

9. SIDS (sudden infant death syndrome) occurs much less often in breastfed babies. Important regulating hormones, such as progesterone, and other infection-fighting chemicals, coupled with the fact that breastfed babies don't spit up as much, may all contribute to why this is so.

10. Breastfeeding is convenient. There are no bottles to clean and sterilize or heat up in the middle of the night. No matter where you go, you always have enough sterile milk for your baby. But remember, whatever you put into your body goes into your milk—such as drugs and alcohol, or prescription medication.

11. Many times babies have allergic reactions to formula and they almost always have a hard time digesting it. These digestion problems can make them uncomfortable and fussier.

12. Breastfeeding can help you get into shape. Extra calories needed for milk production come right off your leftover "baby fat." Your uterus contracts as you breastfeed and returns to its original size. You shouldn't diet while you are nursing, and you also won't have to.

13. Breast milk is free; formula can be quite costly.

14. Much more of the nutrition in breast milk gets absorbed into your baby's body compared to what your baby can absorb from formula. Nature does a better job of making food in a form that your baby can use.

15. Women who breastfeed reduce their chances of getting breast cancer.

16. Recent studies have shown osteoporosis may be less prevalent in women who have breastfed.

17. One of the greatest benefits of nursing is the bond you feel with your baby. Your child feels it and so do you. It's very special.

18. The new guidelines of the American Academy of Pediatrics recommend that infants breastfeed for the first 12 months and that they nurse within the first hours after birth in order to receive the benefits of ingesting the colostrum.

To ensure good milk production make sure you eat a healthy diet. Taking a calcium supplement is also not a bad idea (although don't exceed the recommended dose). Make sure you're getting plenty of iron and enough sleep. In addition, skin to skin contact with your baby will stimulate your body to make milk.

Producing sufficient milk is not usually a problem, but here are a few ways to tell if your baby is getting enough. Your baby should be wetting 6 to 8 cloth diapers a day, a few less if you use disposables, and will have two to five bowel movements a day. Newborns will often nurse as often as every two to three hours (or more). If your baby seems alert when he's awake and is starting to fill out, you should have nothing to worry about. If on the other hand your baby looks more scrawny and dazed than simply lean, and unfocused, check with your pediatrician right away.

If you have discontinued breastfeeding or if you have adopted your baby, you can still nurse. A lactation specialist can help you with the details. The process basically involves stimulating milk production with a breast pump until your body gets the message and produces milk on its own.

Breastfeeding can be especially important if you have a premature or physically sick baby. If your baby is in the hospital you can still nurse. Skin to skin contact and the healing chemicals in breast milk can speed up recovery. Try nursing while you walk your baby around. This movement will keep your baby alert and add to his recovery process.

Every day you breastfeed benefits your baby. Even if you can't imagine nursing until your child decides to give it up, which is ideal, hold out as long as you possibly can. Commit to three months initially, which is a manageable amount of time, and then reevaluate your decision when you reach that date. By that time you and baby will have settled into a routine, your breasts and nipples won't be sore anymore, and the tranquilizing effects of nursing just might have become a benefit you won't want to give up.

Holding and Carrying Your Baby

Kangaroos are one of the few mammals, besides humans, who give birth to extremely underdeveloped babies. Their young are born even more immature than ours, yet the baby kangaroo knows to journey up its mother's belly, drop into her pouch and latch onto a nipple. The mother's pouch is like a second womb and provides the nurturing environment the young joey needs to complete its development. If her newborn didn't find these secure quarters in which to become more stable and self-sufficient, the baby kangaroo would surely become fast food for some predator. But how does this creature, who is no bigger than a peanut, know enough to take the long hike to mother's pouch? Evolutionary trial and error pulled together this combination: nature gave mom the spare compartment, and the newborn the desire to take the trek.

Baby kangaroos instinctively know to crawl into their safety pocket; human infants are programmed to cry for theirs. The survival kit nature has provided for our undeveloped infants is not an instinct, as with the kangaroo, but rather a tool—communication. Our babies cry to be held. If we revere their cries as communications from the design web of species survival, it should have the effect of getting us to carry our babies until they are more developed. We don't have pouches but we do have upright bodies with backs and chests that are well suited for carrying. And we have the intelligence to create our own pouches. (You can choose from a variety of baby-carrying devices these days. They are discussed in more detail at the end of the chapter.)

During their months of life in utero, babies feel the motion of the mother's walk, listen to the rhythm of her heartbeat, and hear the song of her voice. These sensations become imprinted on fetuses and they remember them even after the birth. Being carried reminds babies of that peaceful time in the womb and it helps them feel at ease. Swings and rockers don't really fill the bill because they have an unnaturally even rhythm. Babies know the difference. These devices may work for short periods of time but ultimately they don't supply the human contact your baby wants and needs.

Providing comfort is not the only reason to carry your baby. The rhythm of a person walking, of a heart beating, of breath moving in and out, even the rhythm of someone talking, helps your baby orchestrate all her undeveloped systems. Imagine a band without the band leader and all the musicians play at their own pace and to their own beat. The musicians know how to play their instruments but they haven't learned to play with others. Without a beat to follow, they will produce dissonant and confusing music.

The steady tempo that occurs when carrying your infant pulls all of your developing baby's systems together to make one harmonious sound. You, or whoever else takes care of your baby, become a conductor—a regulating force. When your baby is carried most of the time, she is able to harness your rhythm.

Studies on premature babies show that they do much better when carried frequently. Breathing smooths out more rapidly, digestion is better, mental development is enhanced and they gain weight more quickly. Preemies who are held and carried often leave the hospital sooner and fare better in general than those who are not.

When you wear your baby while doing your work and chores, you challenge her to learn new skills and adapt to novel sensations. Every time you shift positions, lean over, and turn around, your baby needs to balance herself, use her muscles, and refocus her vision. When you wash the dishes, sort through laundry, and go to answer the telephone, your baby is being asked to experience new sights and sounds, to notice cause and effect, to put together meaning and activity. She starts to learn language from hearing you talk. She begins to understand that things open and shut, turn off and on, and that there are so many colors and shapes to study. Because your baby is right there you naturally talk to her and help her to make new connections. This is stimulating stuff that encourages your baby's brain to expand and develop. These simple experiences are entire encyclopedias for your still emerging infant.

Now think about what kind of world your baby experiences inside a crib or playpen. If she is not able to interact with toys yet, there is virtually nothing to stimulate her. She may hear some sounds, see a blur of movement occasionally, but there is no meaning to the experience. A dangling mobile or a picture on the side of a crib is all she has to focus on—not enough to captivate her for long. What is a baby's mind to do with that level of boredom? For the infant who is now mobile it can be even more difficult to be left in a crib or playpen. If she is old enough to play with toys, imagine her frustration at not being able to get to all she can see. Cribs and playpens are like jails. A baby's whole biological, intellectual, and physical being tells her to learn and explore, to be out and about. **Carrying your baby is the best way to stimulate her while keeping her safe.**

But do you really have to carry a baby around so frequently? What are the consequences if one doesn't? For one, your baby will fuss more and expend precious energy and attention in doing so. On the average, a baby who is carried often will cry less than babies who spend their days in infant seats, cribs, and wind-up swings. In addition, when babies are preoccupied with their discomfort, they aren't as available for learning, they have more digestion problems, and irregularities in eating and sleeping.

Survival for a baby means acquiring experience and information, unraveling the mysteries of cause and effect and discovering how things work. These are what will be motivating your child, hopefully for years to come. I say hopefully because the mechanism to explore can be shut down, just like a baby's cry to be held can be shut down.

The crying baby who isn't consistently picked up and carried and stimulated, may eventually learn to stop asking for it. But it doesn't mean everything is fine. She is missing out on what she needs—not extras, not bonuses. Eventually a baby adapts and learns not to be curious, not to want comfort, nor to feel she deserves it. If she is very neglected she learns how not to feel.

You can train babies to lie down in a crib or playpen, to stay with people they aren't attached to, but there are consequences. When babies learn to give up asking for what they need, they soothe themselves by adopting more extreme coping behaviors. These coping behaviors are what become attachment disorders and other dysfunctional behavioral patterns.

Most parents want to give their children the best things that money can buy, but gadgets and gizmos will not replace your baby's need for you. Wind up bassinets and swings, baby gyms, and strollers are all designed to make it easier for parents but they do not always provide what is best for your child. *Things* aren't satisfying for long and depending too much on baby-soothing devices will leave your infant feeling agitated and unfulfilled much of the time. (Doesn't this sound like the state an awful lot of adults are in these days: unfulfilled, bored, and always wanting more things?) There are conveniences of modern infant care that do help busy parents, but they should be used wisely. They should not leave you feeling that being close and involved with your baby isn't important—that *you* aren't important.

The really helpful products on the market are the ones that promote bonding, such as slings and baby backpacks. They're good for baby and free your hands for other work. While carrying your baby you can carry on a business or run errands, do housework and chores or exercise by taking a brisk walk together. If you are a stay-at-home parent, you will be encouraged to get out more, since one baby carrier does the combined job of a stroller, toys, and baby seats (but not car seat). And since your baby is comfortable and happy, she rarely fusses and you aren't frequently unstrapping her out of strollers and seats trying to comfort her.

Baby carriers come in many sizes and shapes with differing needs in mind. Make sure the one you get is comfortable because you will want to use it all the time. Once you see how much happier and calmer your baby is and how much easier your life is, you'll be hooked on wearing your baby.

The sling style carrier can be used to tote your baby in a number of different positions. For one, you can let it hang in the front forming a cozy pouch you have easy access to. And because baby is in a cradled position near your breast, she can also nurse while you are moving about. Also, the absence of any straps or snaps with this style makes it easy to move infants in and out. This convenience is a bonus when you have a newborn who needs to eat and be changed often. The sling style also works well when babies are old enough to be carried on your hip and back.

Another carrier that is useful for newborns and young babies is the front carrying Snugli®. This pouch fits like a knapsack. Straps help distribute the weight and hold the baby close to your body. Your baby is in a more upright position and high enough not to interfere with your walking. Whenever you wear your baby on the front, it is always a good idea to support her head as you bend over and stand up. Little ones can still be a little floppy even in a Snugli®. Also, when you are leaning into something, or turn around quickly, you'll need to remember that your little bundle is there. And be careful when passing by anything hot or working around other hazards.

When your baby is older and heavier, you may want to switch to a backpack type carrier. This style allows your baby to have a wide view of everything around her and she will have more room to stretch her legs. It is also a bit easier to bend over with a backpack, but you will need to be careful that your child is securely fastened and is not going to fly out when you tip forward. In addition, watch out for what your baby has access to from her perch. When she is old enough to reach and grasp, she can grab hold of plants, curtains, curtain chords, lamps, pictures, etc. One time, after a day of shopping, I got home to find that my baby had shoplifted several postcards.

Baby carriers have been steadily gaining in popularity, and it shouldn't be hard to find one at a children's store, garage sale or swap meet. Before you buy, though, try it on and make sure it fits comfortably. Also keep in mind that if dad is going to be carrying the baby, you might want to pick a style or color that will also work well for him.

Like the kangaroos, human babies want to be carried almost continuously until they're a year old. But don't worry about your baby staying in her pouch forever. She will want to move toward her independence as her skills and confidence increase. As baby becomes more mobile, she will fuss to get down and will want more crawling around time. She will want to touch, taste, hold, and shake as many new things as she can. Soon you'll be in the need-to-watch-her-every-second phase, and you'll wish you could contain her again in the safety of your pouch.

Sleep

Sleep becomes a major issue for most parents; they don't get enough of it and their baby seems to be in charge. It is essential that both parents solve whatever problems they are having pertaining to sleep deprivation. Nothing can make a parent more crazed than dealing with work and parenting while under the influence of exhaustion. Beyond simple fatigue, lack of sleep can cause depression, anxiety, and the kind of irritability that can take the roof off. It is a serious problem and not to be taken lightly. It can wreak havoc on your relationships and make parenting feel like torture. **Don't underestimate the effects of sleep deprivation.**

Having said that, how does one get around the fact that newborns need to wake you up every night for feedings, that babies frequently wake themselves up as they move in and out of deep and light sleep, and that children will continue to need you in the night for years to come? There are several answers to that question. First of all, get caught up on sleep whenever you can. Take turns with your mate sleeping in on the weekend, or get a friend, family member or babysitter to watch your child while you take a nap. Get on a schedule that is in sync with your baby. Take naps at the same time and try to get to bed early. Limit your obligations for the first six months so you don't have extra work to keep up with. Forget trying to maintain a perfectly clean house. Eat a healthy diet and cut down on caffeine, sugar and alcohol so they don't interfere with your sleep. These are just a few stop-gap measures. To really deal with sleep deprivation, you have to deal with what's going on with your child.

Many experts recommend that babies get in the habit of putting themselves to sleep so that they can learn to be independent sleepers. Parents are told not to pick up their crying babies when trying to get them to sleep. The theory is that babies gain self-esteem and learn self-reliance by mastering the challenge of learning to "self soothe."

However, you won't find these same experts recommending that your baby try to achieve independence at anything else this young because they know it's not possible. Your baby needs your assistance in every other area of his life, but somehow he is supposed to become accustomed to not needing you at night. The suggestion to condition babies to self soothe may be offered more because of cultural taboos than because it is supported by sound research. Though many pediatricians will recommend solitary sleep for infants, there isn't any research to support this position. We don't really know if this type of sleeping arrangement for infants increases autonomy or increases combativeness and insecurity. In fact, the practice of not attending to your child's security needs in the night is not at all consistent with the latest findings on an infant's need for responsive care.

We know that we do build self-esteem from mastering a challenge. But how are we defining mastery? In part, it involves seeing that a task is attainable, and that we have some ability to accomplish it. It is implied that the act of mastery is difficult but not traumatic. For instance, surviving an ordeal that you are forced to endure may be an accomplishment but it is not mastery. Being put in a situation that is so out of your reach that it's frightening does not build character. Would anyone believe that forcing a crying, pleading, three-year-old to jump off the end of a high dive is going to build his self-esteem? Even if he was made to do it again and again until he got used to it, this would never be a recommended confidence building activity. Would being compelled to engage in an activity that is so difficult it's terrifying, encourage or discourage you? Are you going to resist that activity or engage in it? Evaluating whether or not your child would be experiencing mastery or trauma is one of the questions to concern yourself with when deciding whether or not to condition your child to self soothe.

Dealing with the uncertainties around how to respond to your child in the night is often quite disturbing for most parents. Here are some answers to the most frequently asked questions.

Don't all the latest books on getting your child to sleep through the night recommend that children get in the habit of sleeping on their own and in their own room from the beginning?

The customary arrangement is for parents to create a nursery in a separate room so baby can have peaceful, undisturbed sleep. That way parents get to keep their own space and aren't disturbed either. Many experts recommend that a baby who is old enough to sleep through the night without a feeding should not be picked up if he awakens. Parents are assured that eventually babies learn that no one is going to answer their calls and they will give up and go back to sleep. Recent books that address sleeping problems in children present a more gradual conditioning process but they still require parents to listen to a hysterically crying child and to not pick him up. They can go in and pat him or talk to him at scheduled intervals, but they can not pick him up.

The response I have heard the most from parents who, successfully or not, have used the program, is how badly they felt listening to their babies cry like that. They had to force themselves not to go to them. Even if they fully believed in the legitimacy of the method, it was agonizing for them to hear their child in such distress. One has to wonder, if both parent and child feel so horrible about what's taking place, how can it be the right thing to do?

A common obstacle to resolving bedtime issues is that both parents usually work, are exhausted by the evening and by then want to be free of their children. Teaching children to pacify themselves sounds pretty good to the tired parent. The books that have hit the shelves in the last several years appeal to this exhausted father or mother. The technique they recommend, sometimes referred to as the "cry it out method," has become popular because it does work to some extent. But your child pays a price.

You can force children to change their behavior, but not their feelings or needs. You may not see the immediate risks of using these conditioning programs, but they do exist. Problems can develop later on but by then we will have lost track of the cause. However, it's not too hard to imagine the consequences for a child who repeatedly feels frightened, abandoned or angry—the development of low self-esteem, or a disrespectful disposition is a logical outcome.

You don't need scientists and researchers to tell you what is obvious to every parent. Babies and small children desperately want to be close to a trusted someone in the night because they feel insecure. As a matter of fact, it is of such importance that if you do interrupt the conditioning process just mentioned, and answer their cries, even for one night, children will usually go right back to the original behavior of pleading for their parents to come to them in the night.

Most readers of these books who condition infants find out fairly quickly that there is a significant flaw in "cry it out" programs. They are very difficult to keep up because there are times when you will have to attend to your child's cries in the night, such as when he's sick or wakes up from a nightmare. He will need to be in your bed, or rocked in your arms and before you know it, the conditioning dissolves. It's also true that eventually your child will permanently learn to obey the programming but only after a very long time of reestablishing the pattern over and over again. It is a painstaking process for all.

Getting children to sleep without you is so difficult to achieve and yet so easily undone. That should tell us something about our children's need for nighttime security.

The natural desire of children to need nighttime security most likely originates from our primitive past when the night was truly fraught with danger. In evolutionary terms, nighttime security is a requirement entrenched in our genetic memory. It doesn't matter that you know your child is safe from lions, tigers, and bears; your baby doesn't know it. Even though you may be able to condition your baby to do without you at night, it will not erase that inherited memory.

Here is the key point: your child is extremely helpless and his security needs are high. Babies are programmed to want and need your comfort when they're scared. The question you should ask yourself is what is the appropriate way to treat your child when he is frightened? If a "cry it out" program like the one described is not one you'd put your baby through during the day, what makes it appropriate to use at night?

The difficulty in getting kids off to bed is one of the biggest complaints among parents and it has been for at least as long as the self soothing advice has been around. The problem is that when you do go to your children, say because they are sick or have had a nightmare, you are teaching them that fussing works. Because you can't meet the requirement of never going to your child in the night, you end up creating your own conditioning program. Your child learns that fussing long enough will make you finally come to the rescue. For all the times children are made to settle down on their own, that one time you do go in tells them that ultimately they can make you respond to their need. The end result is that you condition your children into screaming meanies who can go to incredible lengths to get you to stay with them as they try to fall asleep. In the end children who could have outgrown nighttime dependency have become master manipulators who will do anything but go quietly to bed, even well into pre-adolescence.

Some children become conditioned to resist going to sleep; others oppose it because they have learned that bedtime is a negative experience. When babies and small children undergo a lot of crying and apprehension at bedtime, we have defined sleep as something to be dreaded. Instead of fostering *independence* we have increased their insecurity and desire to be *dependent*. We have conditioned them to dislike going to bed.

A child can learn to self soothe but first he or she must be shown how it's done and what it feels like to be soothed. Babies need to gradually learn that sucking and rocking make you feel better. They need to have many repetitions of safe, peaceful sleep in order not to be alarmed when they wake up in the middle of the night. For children to be able to self soothe, they must first experience themselves as potent, successful, and confident individuals. Parents will most likely need to provide for their child's nighttime security for several years before their child can truly achieve nighttime autonomy.

What kind of sleeping arrangements are healthy?

There are a number of different ways to provide for your baby's nighttime security. Some parents put their baby's crib right up against the mother's side of the bed (no cracks in between and wheels locked) with the crib rail down. Because the mattresses are even, pulling the baby in with you to nurse or to provide comfort means you don't have to get up at all. Another arrangement is to simply have baby in bed with you. Best is to have the infant on the mother's side with a safe guardrail securing the outer edge. Usually fathers are equally tuned into their infants when they are in bed with them, but some are not. Mothers tend to be slightly more aware of their child's presence.

The most common fear concerning this arrangement is that you will roll over on your baby. Unless the parents are under the influence of drugs, alcohol, medications, or have medical conditions that would interfere with their normal functioning, this fear is unfounded. If sleeping with your child were that perilous we would never have survived as a species. Shared sleep is what people did for eons.

Recently, several scientific studies have been conducted which demonstrate that shared sleep can be beneficial for your baby. In a series of studies directed by Dr. James McKenna from the University of Notre Dame, and Dr. Sarah Mosko, the sleep patterns of co-sleeping and solitary sleeping babies and their mothers were monitored in a sleep laboratory.

One of the more significant findings to emerge was that babies who slept alone slept deeper and longer than co-sleeping infants. Without the arousal cues and sounds of stirring caused by others in the room, baby's sleep was less interrupted. That may sound like a positive outcome to most parents. However, this type of sleep pattern can cause an infant to experience prolonged pauses in breathing. Their ability to be roused out of a state of sleep, in order to breathe again, can be compromised. It is believed that this pattern of longer, deeper sleep states can be one contributing factor in cases of sudden infant death syndrome. (In fact, in Japan, where co-sleeping is the norm, the incidence of SIDS is very low.)

In another study, McKenna and Mosko found that a baby's physiology changes as a result of co-sleeping. Infants' breathing patterns, heart rate, body temperature, and sleep stages become organized around their mothers'. As a result, their breathing is more regular and their sleep time, although not as deep as solitary sleepers, actually increases.

Another benefit observed in the co-sleeping environment was greater frequency and duration of breastfeeding. Again, this may not, at first, sound like much of a benefit for the mother, but breastfeeding is very protective against SIDS. Although researchers are currently attempting to discover why this may be so, the regulating hormones and natural antibodies found in breastmilk are thought to be at least partially responsible.

Even though an increase in breastfeeding activity during the night would seem to imply less sleep for mother, apparently those fears are unfounded. After a while, breastfeeding can become quite automatic and doesn't require either mother or baby to fully awaken. In fact, in one study, breastfeeding mothers who had their infants with them sometimes slept *better* than mothers who slept alone. And they rated their sleep experience as more positive than the mothers who slept alone.

In addition, when compared with solitary sleepers, co-sleeping infants cried less, bedtime struggles were nonexistent or minimal, and they received more consistent comfort and reassurance.

In an unrelated study, the effects of co-sleeping and solitary sleeping were studied in military families. Far from producing dependent, less mature individuals, researchers found that co-sleeping children received higher ratings on their conduct reports from their teachers and were less likely to require psychiatric care.

These findings shouldn't surprise us. After all, when adaptations were made, it was in the co-sleeping environment. Mothers and babies have been programmed to benefit from this arrangement. Obviously, infants also survive who are off in another room in a crib by themselves—conditions are less perilous now than they were long ago. Nevertheless, it is very significant that co-sleeping has the power to influence an infant's physiology and provide so many benefits.

Although there is much to be learned about co-sleeping, these preliminary studies suggest that nighttime pairing is part of a design package that we would be wise to follow.

Won't having baby in bed with them make sleep more difficult for parents?

Studies show that having your child next to you or in your bed makes it easier for parents to sleep better. When your baby or small child is in the same room and right next to your bed, you can take care of him quickly and easily and you actually preserve sleep. Because newborns have such little stomachs and can only eat a small amount at a time, they may wake up three to four times a night to feed for the first few months. This can be hard on the parents if every time their baby needs them, they have to get out of bed.

Also, when you sleep next to your baby you sleep more soundly because you are aware of his state of health. You don't worry that the sniffle he had during the day hasn't turned into something more serious in the night.

If you hear your baby stirring and starting to awaken, you are right there with a reassuring touch to ease him back to sleep. Neither you nor your child have to become fully roused because baby doesn't get the chance to work up to a full crying session. Your baby will also learn that he doesn't have to be afraid or fussy when he wakes up. He feels secure knowing you're there. The safer your child feels the more he can relax back into slumber.

Isn't it taboo having your baby in bed with you?

For most of our human history children have been sleeping with their parents and, in most of the world, still do. The problem with taboos is that they keep us from speaking the truth. The truth is you should do what you can to reassure your frightened child, day or night. Babies and small children universally feel insecure at night and want to be close to their parents when they go to sleep or awaken in the night. The discrepancy in supporting this taboo is that it runs contrary to not only what scientific studies have shown, but to what most parents would agree is common sense. Conditioning babies to not cry in the face of some very frightening experience is not appropriate. One might even call it cruel.

It's risky to speak out against taboos. The suggestion that parents respond supportively to their children's nighttime fears is bound to be met with some opposition. I have perhaps alienated some of you who find it difficult to question what your pediatrician might advise. However, there are a growing number of child experts who advocate meeting your child's nighttime security needs. They are pioneers of a movement to change this outdated taboo. One of those pioneers is pediatrician Dr. William Sears, who, along with his co-author and wife Martha, recommends that you sleep close to your baby. According to the principles of attachment parenting, providing for your child's nighttime security is simply a matter of continuing with the same level of care as was provided during the day. While parenting eight children themselves, the Sears have experimented with a full spectrum of sleeping arrangements and have experienced first-hand the advantages of shared sleep.

There are a number of sleep configurations that can serve to meet the needs of both parent and child. You might place your baby in bed with you, or put you and your baby in beds side by side, or sleep in your child's room, or have one parent in the guest room and the other in bed with the baby. You may have your baby start out sleeping in your bed and then later transferring him to his own room, or try a combination of all of the above. And arrangements will keep changing as your child gets older and more self-confident. Dr. Sears suggests a family configure whatever arrangements will work best for their particular situation, using attachment parenting as the guide.

Agreeing with a belief does not mean it is simple to embrace. Every family has to decide what they are comfortable with and what seems appropriate. Ultimately, parents need to follow the advice that is best for their particular child, taking into account their unique circumstances.

What about the parents' sex life?

As far as being able to have sex in your own bed, you still can. Put your sleeping baby in another room or on a mattress on the floor next to your bed. Your infant isn't going to "know" what you're doing if he wakes up. If you have an older baby or small child in your room, then go elsewhere. This can be your opportunity to break up the bedroom routine and see what happens when you're in the living room or kitchen. Putting bells on the door where your child is sleeping can alert you that he's awake and on a midnight search. The warning will give you time to pull yourselves together.

This, you may think, will ruin spontaneity and hinder you from just rolling over into each other's arms. It doesn't have to. Your sex life will go through a change anyway as a result of having a child. Like it or not, spontaneity will not be high on the list anymore. If you're too tired to go into another room, then don't. More than likely your sexual time together will be quiet and less energetic. Being tired can have that effect. It's doubtful your sleeping child, whom you can put on a mat and push to another side of the room, is going to hear you anyway.

What this arrangement may require is that you and your mate talk about your sex life, and that may be difficult. You may have to get into the habit of asking each other if he or she is in the mood tonight, something that a touch in the night used to sufficiently convey. Having more communication though, is always a good thing and offers you both an opportunity to get some important feelings out in the open. (See chapter on Sex After Children.)

The only thing I would not recommend is having your children sleeping with you if you are in bed with a date or someone who for all intents and purposes is not your "spouse." First of all, the incidence of sexual abuse is highest with non-parents and step-parents. Secondly, waking next to someone whom your child doesn't consider a full-time parent is not going to feel comfortable. He may not cry about it, but it will still disturb him—as it would you if you were to find someone equally strange in your bed. Better for now to schedule your liaisons to exclude sleep-overs.

Isn't it too much to ask overworked parents to provide nighttime security?

Evening is the time of day when parents are tired and want time off. The pressures on the single family household, whose adult members need to spend many hours commuting and working, is probably why parent advisors continue to extol the virtues of self soothing. Baby's need to feel secure has been superseded by the parents' need for him to be more independent. Parents want the bath, story, and lights out to be accomplished by 7:30 or 8:00 and for that to be the end of it. They're tired and want adult time. Without family or community support parents get few breaks and their desire for private time is understandable. But the irony is that attempts to make baby a self-sufficient quiet sleeper for the parents' sake often backfires. Instead, bedtime becomes notoriously and tortuously a long drawn out ordeal. And for all the maneuvering parents do to get their children to sleep without them, an awful lot of babies and small children end up in their parents' bed or room anyway.

If we still lived in extended families or had communities to back us up, giving our babies a lot of support wouldn't seem so daunting a task. However, in the long run, providing for your child's nighttime security will produce a baby who will demand less of you than one who is always fussy and defiant. Giving your child your love and attention now is not going to drain you nearly as much as living with the consequences caused by an emotionally unhealthy child. Your investment in your child's well-being can mean the difference between having a child you enjoy being with or having a child you are constantly troubled by.

Rather than feeling put upon by having to stay with your child while he falls asleep, incorporate a supportive nighttime routine into your life. For instance, after story time and cuddles are over, you can be reading your own book, listening to music, or sorting the mail while you wait for your child to drift into deep slumber. By staying with your child until he falls asleep, you will actually speed up the bedtime ritual. What is really so wearing on parents is fighting with their children. If your baby doesn't expect to be abandoned, he won't be anxious about giving into sleep.

Won't sleeping in the parents' bed spoil a child or make him or her overly dependent?

In the beginning babies depend on us for their whole existence. We feed, change, hold, and play with them but we don't worry about conditioning them to depend on us to provide these services forever. We are confident that eventually they will learn to feed, clothe and use the toilet by themselves—when they are ready. We know when that is because they show interest and ability in attaining those skills, even if at times we need to help them along. So, is a baby who regularly requires a tremendous amount of reassurance during the day telling us he is ready and able to take on the challenge of independence at night? If babies could talk we would most likely hear—in so many cries—"Are you kidding?"

Nighttime is when babies feel even more frightened and insecure than usual. There are fewer noises and changes of scene to distract them. There are shadows and dark corners they can't see into, and they're too tired to feel easygoing about it. Most babies have already had a full day of trying out new skills and enduring countless frustrations. By evening they naturally feel frazzled. It's your baby's least mature time of the day. This is when baby really needs comforting the most.

Accepting a child's need to depend on you for his security at night is the same as accepting that she has to depend on you during the day. It's true that children will become overly dependent on us if we don't let them experience challenges. They need to have opportunities to test their abilities and cope with their frustrations. But the self-confidence gained from this kind of independence grows from a gradual building of self-mastery, constructed out of daily experiences and over time. It is not a conditioned independence but an earned one. Children do learn to sleep without their parents, when they are ready, and after they have been allowed to gradually master nighttime autonomy. It happens that this can take years because it is actually very difficult to feel secure at night. I know a number of adults who are still uneasy sleeping alone.

What if I never get my child out of my bed?

The fear that you will never get your child out of your room is unfounded. As your child becomes more self-sufficient his security needs lessen. It isn't a coincidence that by the time your child can feed, dress, go to the bathroom, get out his own toys and grab food out of the refrigerator, he is ready to stop needing you as much in the night. By the time he has proven his ability to master problems and meet his own needs, he will be able to cope with sleeping in the dark alone (most of the time).

The trick to nudging your child into his own room is to do it gradually and in small increments. For instance, your child may willingly leave your room if she is gradually encouraged to sleep next to an older sibling, or if she is allowed to have her mattress on the floor (this eliminates fears of falling out of bed or of there being "boogeymen" under the bed). Or to accustom your child to her own room, you might sleep with her every night at first, then every other night, until she feels secure enough to sleep alone. A five-year-old may still want to fall asleep on your bed or with you in the room but gradually can be satisfied by a long snuggling session and a soft music tape.

If, after four to six months, your baby isn't sleeping well (provided there aren't any other extenuating circumstances) here is a list of suggestions or possibilities to consider:

- Have a routine or nighttime ritual such as: bath, chatting, reading, then sleep. Shoot for the same time every night whether it's early or late.

- Check to see if your baby is comfortable. Is he wet, sick, hot, cold, stuffy, or colicky? Does he need burping? Some babies are sensitive to polyester clothing, too much noise or even too little noise, strange sounds, or strong odors.

- Is your baby teething, going through a change in routine, working on a new skill, or dealing with some new kind of stress?

- Is he getting enough to eat? Nurse or give a bottle often during the day so that by nighttime she is well fed.

- Make sure he isn't getting too much sugar; even too much juice at night can make babies hyper.

- Is your baby getting enough of your attention during the day? He might just be missing you. If you are preoccupied or working during the day, he may want more interaction with you before bedtime.

Newborns have to eat when they wake in the night. However, as they get older they get used to this pattern of eating every time they wake up. This conditioning can keep them from going right back to sleep. You may want to see if your baby is willing and able to break this cycle by gradually changing the pattern. Of course step one is making sure your baby is well fed before he goes to bed. Then you slowly set up a new pattern of not feeding your baby every time he fusses in the night.

The first time your older baby wakes up, feed him. The second time, try soothing him by patting his back, singing, or talking in a soothing voice. After several nights (or weeks, depending on the child), instead of feeding him the first time, offer a finger (yours or his) or a pacifier instead. At the same time you might try playing the same quiet music that you use every night when you first put your baby to bed. If you are sleeping next to your baby, have your face close by so he knows you're within reach. Talk to him as you gently rock him back and forth. If he is still crying, pick him up, but don't feed him. Walking and rocking will usually work to get babies asleep again. But make sure he is limp before you put him down again, that way you know he is in a deep sleep. Also, when your baby wakes from naps, don't immediately offer food, unless of course it is clear that he is very hungry. The idea is to break the association of eating with waking up.

It is vital that parents get enough sleep, so it is important that you figure out the arrangement that will help this to occur. I knew someone who occasionally slept at her friend's house while her husband took care of the kids. Another parent often took naps in his office. In our house, my husband and I traded back and forth sleeping with the kids, first in our room, then in theirs.

I knew one single parent who put her child to bed in whatever room she was in at bedtime. The child didn't care what room he was in as long as mom was nearby.

The best sleeping position for a baby is on his side or on his back. The most recent studies on preventing crib death (SIDS) recommend these positions. Don't use too many pillows, mattresses that are too soft, or water beds, and don't have your bed against the wall with baby on that side. These can cause suffocation. Also, don't have your baby sleep right next to another baby or small child, or someone taking anything sedating who could roll on top of him and be too deeply asleep to know it. (Sleeping with a sibling older than six or seven can work with a toddler. This arrangement can help get your toddler out of your room sooner.) Also it is not recommended to have an infant in bed with you if the mother or father smokes.

If you have trouble getting to sleep or staying asleep, even without your baby's interference, you need to get some help. There are now sleep disorder clinics or specialists in most hospitals. Techniques such as biofeedback and meditation or the use of acupuncture, herbal remedies, or homeopathy can also be effective.

Spoiling

A spoiled child is one who is manipulative, clingy, whiney, inconsiderate, destructive, defiant, and/or very uncooperative. Spoiled has been equated with a child who has too much, and yet demands more. He or she screams, cries, argues and does whatever is necessary to be in control. In the past parents have been armed against "giving in to too many of their child's demands" in order to avoid this outcome. They have been led to believe that children are irrational and will always ask for more than is good for them.

Many parents don't understand that much of a child's acting out behavior is a symptom of deeper problems. The child isn't being naughty, she's feeling deficient. A child whose species-specific needs aren't satisfied is more demanding and clingy than one who has been provided with consistent and sensitive care.

This may be hard to believe because it is very different from what parents in the past were told would create demanding, dependent, intolerant and manipulative children.

What does it mean to "spoil" a child?

Spoiling is not caused by always giving in to your child's demands, as most people think. It's more correct to say it's a matter of not setting appropriate limits along with not meeting a child's essential need for consistent and sensitive care. When children's essential needs for nurturing are not respected and supported, they become demanding. Their needs don't go away and they are angry about their discomfort. They feel out of control because they have failed to get what they require to feel secure and stimulated. They must work even harder at maintaining control because they feel their safety depends on it. Unfortunately this also means resisting parental authority, throwing tantrums, and being demanding, and manipulative just so they can feel securely in charge.

Spoiled children:

- Are often insecurely attached to their primary caretaker(s).

- Have been given *things* (toys, cookies, more TV) instead of attention. No matter how much you give them, they always wants more. That's because *things* don't satisfy their hunger for a secure bond.

- Haven't had limits set around destructive, unhealthy, and rude behavior. They are allowed to talk back, hit,

tease, hurt, eat junk and, in general, act disrespectful-
ly to people or property.

- Are overprotected and have not been given the opportunity to discover or do anything for themselves. The
caretaker has kept them from taking risks and learning new skills. They don't develop self-confidence and
instead learn they are helpless. As a result, they feel
insecure and unfulfilled, leading them to act demanding and controlling.

- Have been exposed to negative role models on TV, or are
around people who act aggressively and uncooperative-
ly. Children primarily learn by imitating what they see.
If you or anyone else in your child's world (including
TV characters and playmates) is acting "spoiled," then
your child will learn to act that way as well.

Setting appropriate limits is absolutely necessary and must
be done firmly and consistently, but that doesn't necessitate parents acting punitively and unkindly. You don't have to sound or
act mean for a child to take you seriously. As a matter of fact,
with the younger child, you need to speak with love, patience and
understanding. You don't cave in to your child's demands or
undo a limit you or your mate have set forth, but neither do you
have to shame your child or yell at him.

Do not allow your child to manipulate you into changing
your mind by throwing a tantrum. If you've said no to the
candy, the soda, the violent TV show, if you've set a rule that
they can not hit you or scream to get their way, do not waver
from this stance. If you give in, you will teach your children
that they can hold you hostage and get their way. Do not let
your children take control in these matters (again, we are not
talking about species-specific needs).

If they are toddlers, use humor or distract them. Children are very strong-willed at this age but they are also very willing to replace one form of fun with another. Your job is to find a worthy replacement for their present fixation. Almost always, a parent acting silly or talking in a funny voice will do the trick. Even so, they may cry and object, so let them know you understand that it's hard for them not to always get what they want. You can empathize with their unhappiness, but firmly let them know that it will not make you change your mind.

As children get older, distractions will no longer be appropriate. Explanations will be more suitable. Tell them why you have set the limit one, two, maybe three times, but no more. Your child demanding that you continuously justify your decisions is not appropriate. Tell your child that you have said all that is necessary and you will not be talking about it further. Ignore any more questions. Make sure you have made yourself clear, however, before taking this stand.

Children need to feel that *you* are in control in order for *them* to feel safe. They want to know that someone is in charge who is more knowledgeable and confident than they are. Children ultimately want their parents to have the last word. Even the strong-willed child who pushes back every time you say no, needs boundaries to be firmly set.

In general, say yes to security and stimulation and no to disrespect, danger, angry destructiveness, and unhealthy influences.

How does a child become more independent and what can parents do to help?

Parents need to encourage their children to test their independence, but they need to be sensitive to their particular child's capabilities. The depth of your child's cries and pleas will clue you in. You will sense when your child is being pushed too far, too fast. In general, however, your children's desire to grow up and be in charge of their own lives far outweighs their desire to maintain a dependency that is no longer needed.

The key phrase here is *no longer needed*. When children have enough experience under their belts and have successfully mastered one stage, they are ready, willing, and able to move on to the next. If we traumatize them or push them too hard, they will hold on for dear life.

If anything, the journey children are programmed to take, now and for the rest of their lives, is to *individuate*. They go from being part of your body while in the womb, to becoming a separate person at birth. They advance from being carried in your arms, to toddling, to running off. They go from sleeping in your bed to going to school and pretty soon they'd rather be with friends than with you. Children do not prefer dependency over independence, but they aren't going to give up their security until they feel safe and capable. If we allow our children to set the pace, they will test their wings when they're ready, and we will have to let them fly. **The rule of thumb is to not do for your children what they can do for themselves.** Until they can do more for themselves, we must provide for their feeling of security.

The difficulty adults have is realizing just how long it takes for a human being to mature, how long we, as parents, need to act as a secure base and respectful facilitator. Human beings require eighteen years to mature. At least half that time is a period of primal development, and, even then, a nine-year-old is just barely competent to make thought-out decisions which consider past events weighed against future consequences. Impulse control is still limited, as is the ability to act responsibly. It will take six to nine years for your baby to reach minimum maturity. That is why children need a lot of security for the first three years—because they are literally helpless and at your mercy.

Sometimes we misinterpret normal dependency, which is tied to a biological clock, for "spoiled dependency." Yes, our children change daily and seem to grow so quickly, but we forget to measure that progress against how very far they have to go before they are capable of independence. Parents are in a jet stream world compared to their child's snail's pace unfoldment. We are a fast track society and it is difficult to adjust our pace to that of nature's. Resist trying to make your child independent before she is naturally capable of it.

How do we know when to protect and when to let go?

Your child will tell you. For instance, if you put your baby down to sleep in your bed, then later carry her into her crib, and she wakes up crying frantically in the night, your baby's message is that this is too scary an arrangement. Maybe a slower transition is in order. Children tell you how much psychic pain they are in with the intensity of their feelings, which includes being intensely withdrawn. Your child's extreme reactions, other than natural traits of temperament, can represent her most important communication—all is not well.

Likewise, if we never give children the opportunity to explore and try out new skills, they will never be ready to move on and they will act whiney and clingy. We stunt their growth when we prevent them from carrying out *their* attempts to individuate. When we deny them their choices and their attempts at discovery, we take away their self-confidence. If we discourage a baby's attempts at exploration and discovery, he will internalize it as a message that he is incompetent. Babies naturally want to explore and discover, which often gets them in trouble. Parents can be too smothering if they don't allow their babies safe ways to test their limits.

When do you say no?

Discipline doesn't really come into play until the second year. Obviously you will be having to direct your mobile infant before that time, but that is different from expecting your baby to *learn* how to behave differently. Babies under a year old will continue to pull the books off the shelves every day no matter how many times you say no. The trick is to remove the books from their reach. Into the second year the toddler can begin to make some connections, but their impulse control still will be quite limited. It will work better to redirect your two-year-old than to say no, or expect him to have self control.

Setting limits is very important, especially around anything concerning danger and disrespect. However, setting limits around nurturance and security is not appropriate. The kinds of situations you want to save your struggles for are when they:

- Intentionally hurt animals, people, or damage property
- Want to eat too much junk food
- Are rude, disrespectful, and unkind
- Constantly demand that you buy them things
- Insist on being exposed to unhealthy influences (violent, disrespectful TV and video shows, etc.)
- Are doing something dangerous

• Need to cooperate with you (such as when it's time to leave the park, go to bed, etc.)

When you do have to set limits in these areas, make sure you teach your child about what he is doing wrong or needs to do right. For instance, it is normal for toddlers to act aggressively. They don't yet understand the consequences of their actions. If your toddler hits another child you need to tell him, "You are hurting your friend. That's not okay. Tell her you're mad. But no hitting." You might want to model for your child how to talk to her friend such as saying, "I'm mad because you took my toy away. Don't do that." You want your child to start understanding why you say no and how to deal with his frustration. Wherever possible model the appropriate behavior. That's how children learn correct social skills. Teach them as early as possible how to communicate what they feel.

Tell your child why you're setting the limit by using short phrases. If your toddler won't go to bed you might say something like, "You need sleep to feel good. When you're tired you feel bad and want to cry a lot. That's no fun." Toddlers understand basic concepts like good and bad, pain and fun. They can begin to see cause and effect in these terms.

Whenever you discipline your children, don't ever use shame as a way of getting them to "learn their lesson." The only thing they will learn is how to have low self-esteem. No one learns to be a better person by first feeling that they are a bad person. Phrases such as, "How could you do that? Shame on you," and "You are a very bad boy," are not useful. Shame doesn't work to modify behavior. If you feel you are a bad person you also feel impotent, stupid, incompetent, hopeless, and defeated. These are not emotional states that encourage one to feel they can and want to change. Better you use the opposite tactic and say things such as, "I know you will do better next time," and, "You made a mistake and everyone makes mistakes. You're a smart boy. I bet you're not going to do that one again." Positive reinforcement works the best to modify behavior. For more information on this, order my booklet, *Disciplining Your Small Child.*

PART TWO

Family Life

Dads
(please read)

A dad's reactions to having a baby may be a little different from the mom's. Built into men is a survival mechanism that tells them to feel responsible for providing food and shelter. This may sound sexist, but it's not. It's simply a general statement about the genetic instructions men have been given, a description of the evolutionary design that has assisted our survival for many thousands of years. Men needed to develop strengths, aggressions, and instincts in order to do what was necessary to ensure that their offspring survived. While mothers were busy nursing and caring for the children, somebody had to get food and protect the family—the father. This was a system that worked well for a long time and only recently has needed revising. It may be an obsolete configuration now but the genetic coding is not. Men are inclined to be hunters. Even though these inherited instructions don't eliminate other possible scenarios (women can survive on their own and men can be nurturers), nevertheless, many new fathers experience a nagging burden to be providers. Some men will feel confident about meeting the challenge. Others will be anxious and tense because they feel insecure or inadequate about helping their little one survive.

Ultimately, the anxiety is constructive because it creates an urgency in men to provide for their child. But what happens when men don't know how to respond to these new feelings of restless agitation? What happens when they don't have healthy role models available—grandfathers, uncles, their own and other fathers—to act as mentors? When new fathers today experience anxiety about their new role, they are often unaware of where it's coming from and they have little support and guidance to help them. Fatherhood can be daunting—even frightening.

The instinctual response to fear is **fight or flight.** One either dominates the source of the threat to him, or tries to escape it. Overall it's an effective knee-jerk response, a good survival mechanism, but not one that should be directed toward one's family. Sometimes the unconscious response of men is to do battle with their insecurity by working longer and harder at their jobs, maneuvering for more money, power, or job security. Or they become chronically angry, defensive, or abusive (fight). On the other hand, some men may become depressed, turn to alcohol, drugs, thrills, other women, divorce, or whatever helps them to avoid their fear and anxiety (flight).

Those aren't the only choices men have—they can also call upon creative problem solving, and basic higher brain functioning to grapple with their fears. They don't have to rely on instinct to guide them. Unlike babies, men can choose to rethink the evolutionary messages they've been given. However, if there isn't a cultural standard of behavior to follow or good role models and support systems in place, how else can a man act but instinctively?

It is a difficult time for men these days. Their roles have drastically changed since hunting-gathering days. They are being asked to interact in ways that are very unfamiliar to them, feel in ways they are unprepared for, and do it with minimal support.

Women have their own battles, but they are different ones. Women have maintained many of the roles they were wired for—creator of life, nurturer, healer, food manager, homemaker, worker—but men live in a totally different world. They do few of their former jobs (or do them only in their spare time) like hunting and fishing for sustenance, building shelter, observing and learning from the natural world, inventing tools, and relying on their own two feet to get them where they need to go. Not that life for primitive men was always predictable and within their control. There were droughts, harsh winters, sickness, and starvation, but even with those calamities, survival was primarily the *direct* result of a man's labor.

Instead of having the means within their grasp to ensure the survival of their families, men today have to rely on a multitude of strangers, machines and ever-changing complex systems to do the work for them. So many elements in a man's life are out of his control—bosses, clients, economics, cars, corrupt politicians, the unpredictable behavior of reckless drivers, greed, and random violence are just a few of them. Men are no longer directly in charge of life's basic necessities. Survival is based less on their mastery and skill and more on the good will of others and good luck.

What a predicament for men to be in. Not only are they unable to rely on themselves, but their genetic coding tells them not to trust others unless they are in your clan. But few men today have a circle of trusted male friends they can rely on and they almost never have a community behind them. Under such conditions it is natural for a man to be suspicious, afraid of intimacy, and defensive. These traits, however, are not conducive to sustaining a family today.

More than ever before men need the support of friends, family, and community to help allay their fears of having so little control over their survival. Men need to feel they have allies when the insecurity gets to be too much. But for the most part men live in an unpredictable wilderness—alone. The lack of support they have in their lives is a monumental problem and dramatically affects their emotional health and well-being.

Typically, new fathers act like their own fathers did, which too often means "flight"—being absent emotionally if not literally. Most of the time they act on instinct and continue to imitate the behaviors they have been exposed to. Between the kind of modeling they received growing up, economic pressures to make money, the cultural pressure to look successful/feel successful, and the overall acceptance of divorce, men don't have a lot of encouragement for becoming involved fathers. Sadly, years later, these same men often look back and regret they missed so much of their child's life.

The best encouragement for a father to become more involved comes from bonding with his child. The love and protection a man feels for his child will give him the courage and perseverance to get through his fear and anxiety. If the father is involved from the beginning of the pregnancy, by the time the baby is born, bonding will already be in progress. A baby will respond to his father's voice soon after birth. It isn't long before the child recognizes the dad's face and delights in his attention.

This bond is what will help a man find whatever solution is needed to keep his family intact. When dads are securely bonded with their children, fight and flight are less viable options.

Balanced priorities and secure surroundings become the goals that make the most sense. Higher brain functioning instead of instincts drives decision making.

Forty percent of all children are growing up without their biological father. Recent studies into teen violence cite the absence of a father as the major contributing factor in teen delinquency. These are very important statistics. Dads who are too busy with their work, or who divorce themselves from their families, are leaving holes in their child's emotions that can have devastating consequences.

When children of divorce grow up they often deal with their pain by erecting emotional barriers and never getting close to others. They fill the void by compensating with money and things, or replenish their emptiness with addictions, gang "families," violence, or thrills. They seek relief from their anger and grief, but most of the time their coping mechanisms are self-destructive.

A common reason why a dad begins to distance himself from the family is because he and the mom aren't getting along. (The section "Keeping Your Relationship Together" will go into this more.) You both may be cranky from lack of sleep, you're overworked, your nerves are frayed. Tempers can flare quickly. The two of you begin fighting more and pretty soon dad is getting a beer after work, hanging out more with the guys, or becoming lost in sports, hobbies, or work.

Family life is chaotic and tense at times. Feuding is a reality that must be dealt with head on and the issues resolved, otherwise they will become the wedge that comes between a man and his family.

Sometimes dads are less involved with their child because the mom, consciously or not, pushes him out. Mom takes over too many of the bonding activities. She is always the one comforting baby when he's fussy and needs changing. She does the burping, feeding, and reads the bedtime stories. Dad doesn't end up bonding with the baby because mom doesn't make enough room for him. He isn't made to feel important, competent, and needed. She may criticize the dad's awkwardness or inefficient handling of the baby and think it would be easier to do it herself. Or she may resent all the work she has to do and blame the dad for not doing enough. This puts dad in a no-win situation because he can never do anything right. Instead of asking for what she wants, the mother yells at her mate, blaming him for many of her problems. However, her anger only makes it more difficult for dad to get close to her and the baby.

Sometimes when mom does vent her frustration at dad it is because she too is overwhelmed by her new role as parent. She feels afraid and inadequate and takes it out on her partner. But her anger keeps the father from connecting with his child and being a support to the family.

Dads give their children unique experiences that are not as much about gender as they are about revealing another view of life. Dads experience challenges and stress differently. What excites them, what they wish for, what they reinforce and awaken in their children will be different than what their children get from mom. Dads offer an alternate experience that rounds out a child's understanding of what life is all about. The child learns that there are any number of possibilities and ways of perceiving the world.

Fathers contribute to the formation of their children's self image. Children feel valued when they are validated and appreciated by someone they feel connected to. As children grow they need to know themselves through another's loving eyes, like those of their parents. A father's approval, recognition and encouragement literally help define a child's self image.

Lastly, from observing parents together, children learn about the give and take involved in daily conflicts, and how to resolve these conflicts. They learn about relationships from two points of view. They learn about cooperation, companionship and sharing, they see the mixing of strengths and the mirroring of reactions. They learn social skills—among the most important for a child to learn.

Can a child thrive without a father? Yes, but it would matter why and how. Sometimes dads die; with adopted children, neither biological parent is around. As is the case of gay couples, dad is not even the right word to describe the other parent. But a gay co-parent is as vital as a biological father. All that child needs is to feel securely bonded to the person whom they have come to know from the beginning as the other parent. Gay parents turn out perfectly healthy children—which only validates the importance of a secure bond as the primary factor in a child's emotional health. If anything, our reactive societal attitudes toward gay parents, mixed race families, or anyone we are prejudiced against, is what undermines the health of children.

What can be very damaging for a child is when there is a dad who could be in the picture but isn't, because the parents are divorced or separated. The baby or child experiences abandonment. Some children will eventually work through their feelings, others will not and they may always have some emotional problems because of it. When a dad leaves or is never around, children feel as if the problems were their fault, perhaps thinking that they weren't worth taking care of. When someone you love doesn't spend time with you, it's difficult not to think, "She just doesn't want to," or "I must not be good enough for him." Babies and children need you to maintain your connection with them to demonstrate that they are worthwhile.

Except for breastfeeding, dads should follow the same guidelines to bonding with their babies as moms. They need to be holding, carrying, feeding, and tuning into their baby just as much as the moms. They need to follow the practices of responding to their baby's cries, making eye contact, playing, and soothing their child, and doing what they can to help the family run smoothly.

There is no getting around the fact that for the first couple of years, children need a lot of attention and require sacrifice. But it won't last forever. Listening to crying, not being able to go out whenever you want, having more work to do—this is hard stuff. But it's worth it, because raising a child is an incredible experience. Understanding and addressing the cause of your stress, instead of avoiding it, is what will make you feel better—leaving your family won't.

If you are a father who is starting to pull away from your family, it's important that you do something to reverse the process right away.

Here is a list of practical suggestions to help you feel more connected, relaxed and in control.

1. Develop a trusting relationship with your mate and one other person. Be open with them and share your anxieties and upsets.

2. Invent—take up a hobby, a challenge, an artistic endeavor that demands your creativity and ingenuity. Engage in it when it doesn't interfere with family responsibilities, such as in the evening when you would normally be watching TV or going out.

3. Get healthy—find a middle ground in whatever your

vices are—sugar, caffeine, work, alcohol, TV watching, tobacco, etc.

4. Get exercise. Do something you enjoy. Or try something new—mountain biking, hiking, tennis, canoeing. Better yet, get a baby stroller that you can push while jogging.

5. Challenge yourself. Learn a language, learn carpentry, learn how to swim; do something you don't feel "good" at. Mastering a difficult skill is good for your self-esteem and genetic urgings.

If you are having a hard time because you're unemployed, depressed, having problems in your relationship, or if you're fighting an addiction, get help. Being a dad means you put the needs of your child first for a while and do whatever it takes to solve your problems.

Addictions are especially damaging. High doses of alcohol, drugs, gambling, sex, or work may seem to provide an escape and perhaps for a while you won't care about your problems. But they will catch up with you—the higher you go the farther you fall. In the long run, addictions end up costing you a lot: in money, relationships, self-esteem, energy, and enthusiasm. Addictions put you on an emotional roller coaster which only adds to your stress. You have something valuable to contribute to your child's life. Don't let an addiction, or depression or other debilitating feelings get in your way. Get the support you need—and deserve.

Keeping Your Relationship Intact

Hopefully there are two of you parenting this child and sharing in the diaper changing and sleepless nights. Not that single parent homes can't be successful. Those parents should be applauded and given huge helpings of support. Certainly, healthy, wonderful children come out of families of every shape and size. But the reality of raising a child is that it's a lot of work and it takes several devoted, loving adults to do the job in such a way that no one gets burned out. If the adults aren't overwhelmed and overly committed, the kids are more likely to be well tended to. It's not the configuration of the family that counts but how secure and bonded the children feel, which includes having healthy parents.

What matters is that the care is secure, consistent, and sensitive to the child's needs, and that's very difficult to do alone. If at all possible, parents should try to raise their child together simply because it is the arrangement that works best for all (unless the family environment is abusive).

The Consequences of Divorce

When a child's bond with a parent is severely disrupted, it can result in an attachment disorder or other long term emotional and behavioral problems. Divorce often damages that bond. Some kids survive intact, but the majority of children have problems later in life. It's not always possible, or even desirable for two people to stay together, such as when there is abuse, violence, or dangerous addictions, but otherwise divorce should be the very last resort when there are children involved.

As a culture, we value choice and have fought hard for our freedoms. We want to be able to change our mind, change our lifestyle, or change partners, if that's what we think is in our best interests. But along with freedom of choice goes taking responsibility for our actions. Once you have children, their needs take priority. Fortunately, if you commit completely to a relationship, it is easier to resolve your differences, and many problems disappear.

Divorce is a big part of our culture. We don't like to admit that there is anything wrong with it—and there isn't, except when children are involved. Recent studies have shown that the children of divorce:

- Have a high rate of divorce themselves
- Have a high rate of substance abuse
- Tend to have low self-esteem

• Tend to be co-dependent

• Have difficulty making commitments

• Become over or underachievers in the extreme

• Often develop obsessive-compulsive disorders

• Usually are mistrustful

There are a number of scenarios which put children at risk and that accompany most separations and divorces:

• The absence of a parent feels like abandonment.

• The disrupted bond creates fear and anxiety in the child.

• Just being in the same room with fighting parents makes children feel like the yelling is being directed at them.

• Both parents usually become preoccupied with themselves and pay less attention to their child.

• One or both parents may become depressed. As a result they not only are less available for their child but they will typically exhibit an expressionless face, which babies especially find very upsetting. A depressed parent is a major cause of attachment disorders.

• Parents may start to resent their child because they feel he or she is the cause of their problems.

• The child is resented because he or she looks like the other parent.

• The majority of children of divorce grow up in poverty and subsequently receive substandard childcare, medical care, etc.

• Children have to cope with very confusing and inconsistent environments, which is frightening, disorienting and ultimately very stressful.

When you divorce your mate, you also leave your child. For a small child who does not have a full grasp of time, a week between visits can be a lifetime and a serious disruption to the parent/child bond. Maintaining that bond requires consistent attention that the absent parent can't provide. It does matter what a parent tells the child about why he or she is leaving (if the child is old enough to understand), but the child may still feel he or she is also being divorced. Younger children, especially, experience themselves as the center of their universe. They see themselves as the cause for all that happens to them. Divorce often makes them feel like they did something wrong.

Fighting

The problems that develop in a relationship usually happen slowly. If the couple doesn't communicate well, if they haven't periodically engaged in mutual marriage maintenance, they can get into trouble before they know it. These are distracting times and it's easy to get caught up in a whirlwind of activities that take our focus away from our relationships. When trouble brews we can live with it for a long time before we realize just how much distance has developed between ourself and our mate. While we carry on with all the other details of our life, we work around the tensions that are so hard to face.

Then behaviors shift a notch—usually intensifying. Arguments increase or silence deepens; the problems become more intrusive and too disturbing to ignore. At this stage, the couple's relationship will have already sustained significant damage. The distance that has developed between them makes cooperative endeavors of any kind unlikely. If drastic measures aren't taken soon (such as seeing a counselor), this couple may be on the road of no return. If animosity continues for too long, wounds can become too deep to heal.

The real reason most couples fight is because they are acting out the pain they experienced during childhood. That may sound like old-time psycho-babble, but it's true and exactly the point why this book is so important. Those childhood wounds stay with you and often never heal, even with therapy and medication. They become the landscape of your life. Sometimes the only possible way to heal is to acknowledge their existence and to learn to work within your limitations. You find ways to accept and appreciate your strengths but you also learn to skirt around, under, and through the rest. The damage itself doesn't heal. The anger, hurt, and fear never completely go away, and we have unhealthy residues that pop up and interfere with our relationships.

For the record, most of our anger at another does not fit the crime. Most of us unfairly blame others, in particular our spouses, for having caused our upsets. When you are angry at your mate you need to realize that you are probably more angry then you should be due to your tender scars. You are in effect getting your buttons pushed and you are overreacting.

If you unfairly vent your frustrations at your spouse then you need to acknowledge your part and apologize.

All of us are pretty self-righteous when we're angry and we exaggerate our injuries. Marriages require that both people get off their high horse and learn to apologize and forgive each other DAILY! It's one of the cornerstones of maintaining a healthy partnership.

The three statements to say to your partner that will keep your relationship thriving are:

1. I appreciate you.

2. I'm sorry.

3. I forgive you.

If you are committed to a healthy relationship, these words will need to be part of your vocabulary on a regular basis. The reason why these statements are so powerful is because they contain the key elements required for emotional health. We need: to feel valued, to take responsibility for our actions, and to heal each other's shame by accepting that we all make mistakes. **Being in a marriage means that you try to help your partner to be as healthy as possible.**

Coexisting peacefully is not easy for anyone and we seem to be getting worse at it. Maybe it's because we don't understand the importance of commitment and of these three simple phrases: I appreciate you; I'm sorry; I forgive you. We aren't taught them in school; we didn't see our parents use them, and television rarely models such exchanges. Yet these statements form the foundation of any close relationship.

You will not work hard at the problems that you face in your relationship unless you are committed to your partner. If, in the back of your mind, you think, "I don't have to put up with this," then you already have one foot out the door. Begin with the assumption that this marriage is it—you are in for the long haul—for better or worse. If you assume the only relief to your anger and frustration is to better the marriage, then you will find a way to do so. Commitment to your marriage will give you the motivation to go beyond what you perceive are your limitations.

New Expectations

Conflict and disagreements are normal but having a baby can turn up the heat. Parenthood can be very hard on a relationship. By definition, the focus shifts from the couple to the baby and toward the process of becoming a family. As a result, the couple needs to redefine expectations. Before children, a couple had many more choices for reducing stress and finding entertainment. Options of lifestyle, as well as future plans were open-ended. Now the allotted portion of time over which the couple has control has just shrunk considerably. Not only do they have less romantic time with each other, but they have less time for themselves. This is not an easy adjustment to make.

Guess who is going to bear the brunt of your frustration? That's right, your mate. If you are frustrated and tired enough, you will want to blame your partner for just about everything. Some of those frustrations however, will be stemming from your non-acceptance of the new arrangements. Most of the time you will be unaware of how the increase of stress in your life is causing you to be more irritable and intolerant.

Having a baby doesn't mean that now you get nothing for yourselves, but the form of your good times will have to change. Much of your fulfillment and joy will need to come from activities you do together as a family. You will of course want to set some time aside for yourselves to be alone and with each other, but mostly you will want to integrate new forms of entertainment into your lives—family oriented fun. Playing games, doing puzzles, and having potlucks are a few examples of family style entertainment.

Surviving the stresses of parenting with your family intact is going to take effort and a dynamic approach. Too often we let life happen to us rather than taking the reins in hand. Instead of creating the life we want, we feel like victims, scorned and let down. We let our relationships spiral out of our control. We add insults to injury until the relationship self-destructs.

Don't let this happen to you. **Commit** to working out your problems—it's the first and most important step in building a strong foundation for any relationship. You are with your mate for a reason. There is an important tie between you. Maybe you have discovered some traits you find undesirable or out and out intolerable. The ones that aren't destructive to you, you just may have to accept as part of the package deal. So your partner is messy, picky, grouchy, or insensitive. Patiently and with kindness, work out some compromises. Actively look for solutions.

When you are feeling fatigued and angry, try not to take it out on your partner. Better to scream into a pillow than at your spouse. Tell him or her *what* you are feeling, instead of inappropriately unloading your frustrations. For example, say things like, "I feel so overwhelmed by how much we have to give to this baby," or "I am so tired I just can't take you asking me for anything right now," or "I know you're feeling frustrated but please don't yell at me." Communication is the key to sidestepping your irritation. **Say what you're feeling instead of acting it out.**

Try to identify what the biggest source of your stress is. Is it financial worries, feeling like you have too much to do, or feeling burdened by your baby? Are one or both of you depressed? Or worse, are you abusing drugs, alcohol or each other? If any of these is the case, don't be afraid to get help. You can break the cycle. Your lives can change dramatically for the better, if you get help. As a counselor, I can tell you that I've seen relationships turn around hundreds of times. You don't know what is possible until you've tried. So what have you got to lose but your bad feelings?

The guiding principle to keep in mind is to continually work toward feeling connected, as a couple and as a family. If you can talk about your problems and search *together* for a solution, you will maintain that connection. There is so much that separates us these days: work schedules, commutes, errands, appointments, meetings, even societal pressures to always increase what we earn and spend; the complexity of our lives is astonishing. Tragically, families may spend little time together—if they don't watch it, they will grow apart. My booklet, *Eight Steps to a Better Marriage* can help you work on and maintain your relationship.

Many relationships sour that don't have to. The ingredients to happiness were there—the couple just didn't know how to deal with destructive anger and frustration. If you commit to staying connected as a family your feelings of intolerance will be tempered and your willingness to look for solutions will expand. **Life conforms to your expectations.** If you make having a good marriage a definite goal, chances are that is exactly what you will get.

Difficulties are going to come up. The more you are willing to accept that, the easier it can be to get through them.

Sex After Children

One of the more difficult changes, for some couples, that occurs after having children is a dramatic drop in the frequency of sex. Women may have less desire due to a hormonal shift that results from giving birth and the vaginal soreness that can accompany it. If an episiotomy was performed after the delivery, it can be too painful to have sex for a number of weeks. However, fatigue is often the biggest culprit for a drop in libido and sometimes it can take its toll for years. Sleep deprivation, working full time, or just the rigors of taking care of a baby can make you exhausted. After you've been giving to your baby and/or job all day long and repressing your own needs in the process, the last thing you want to do is to meet your partner's needs in bed. By the end of the day you are tapped out and don't need more stimulation. If you've been with your baby all day long, you probably have had enough touching. By evening you just want to vegetate.

Whatever the reason, it is normal, especially for women, to lose a large percentage of their sex drive for a while, and there isn't a lot that can be done. Husbands can, of course, help to reduce their wife's work load. Women can make sure that they get all the rest they can, but usually the frequency of lovemaking decreases anyway. To some extent men need to recognize this and be patient and accepting of the situation.

However, there are some arrangements that the couple can work out to make this time more bearable. Frequency may drop, but quality doesn't have to. The following are a few suggestions to get you moving in the right direction:

1. Take baby over to the house of a friend, family, or babysitter. Instead of going out, stay home for a romantic evening together.

2. When having a romantic evening, make it as much like a date as possible. Put on sexy clothes and underwear, fix your hair, shave, etc. Plan to have a sensuous meal for just the two of you. Get good take out food and bring it home so that less time is spent on shopping, cooking and cleaning up. After dinner put on some soft music and dance in the living room, slowly undressing each other as the night progresses. Next head for a warm bath by candlelight or to the bedroom for a session of mutual massage. After that, do whatever comes naturally.

3. If you can't arrange for a date, remember to still leave plenty of transition time before having sex. It's difficult for most women (and some men), who have just spent the evening being a parent, to go straight from diaper changing to frolicking in bed. Spend sufficient time on foreplay. The most instant body relaxer is massage. Use oil or lotion to add to the sensuous feel. Slow even strokes feel the best. This isn't the time to work out muscle knots with deep pressure. The point is to awaken sensual pleasure in the body. And remember to do the hands and feet; these areas can often be the most stimulating.

4. The more tantalizing you can make the moment the better. Slow everything down—every touch, every move. Enliven your senses. Give the least amount of stimulation possible. Let the anticipation build. Don't focus on having an orgasm. Focus on the thrill of your partner's touch. If you want to increase the sexual tension, deny yourselves intercourse for awhile, and just engage in foreplay.

5. Some couples I have talked to have developed a style of lovemaking designed to deal with the problem of one partner being less sexually turned on than the other. In essence, the ones desiring sex derive their satisfaction from giving pleasure to their partner. They assume the active role. The passive partners have only to receive the touches and caresses. They are not expected to "satisfy" their partner in return. Usually the passive partner perks up and becomes a more active participant, but the important point is that they aren't expected to. It is a marvelous thing to learn how to purely give and purely receive pleasure.

The point of these suggestions is to help you find ways of dealing with your new life. Learn how to enjoy less energetic sex, give massages often, and focus on touch and intimacy more than intercourse and orgasm. Enjoy the excitement of a stolen moment in the kitchen, a sexy whisper in the ear, a tender kiss on the neck. Actually, sex after kids can be as exciting as when you were virginal teenagers.

Returning To Work

Although my bias is to put children's needs first, which to me means having one parent home for the first year, I recognize the health of the family as being an integral part of what influences the healthy development of the child. Usually, both parents have to work just to meet their bills, which obviously takes priority. Poverty can have a very negative effect on a baby, not the least of which is the stress it puts on the parents. But it would seem that an awful lot of families are dissatisfied with the choices they've been given. They are feeling stretched to the limits and are very stressed out by the kind of lifestyle they have been forced to adopt. Most working parents don't feel they ever spend enough time with their children, and they're probably right. If it were left to them—they would be home with their baby.

In the past it has been extremely nonproductive, even destructive, to attribute the cause of all our children's faults to the inadequate care given in families. It is inaccurate to blame the downfall of the family on women's liberation and their desire to pursue meaningful careers. Nor is it useful to ascribe the cause to parents who are too self-involved, or to climbing divorce rates, the pursuit of affluence, or any other reason that originates within the family. This kind of finger pointing is one-sided and never exposes the whole picture. We live in a larger family, that of our society.

If there are any entities responsible for defining our choices, shaping our reactions, and molding our environments, they are government, the media, and the business community. They are the ones with the power to define what is possible for families to achieve. They are more responsible than single individuals in ultimately stacking the deck in favor of the healthy or unhealthy development of a child. They are very influential in defining the kinds of stress and quality of care that are available to children via their parents.

This book is not designed to address these issues but it is important for all of us to stop adapting and start objecting to the unacceptable lifestyles which families are forced to adopt. A wonderful organization called Healthy Families Partnership assists individuals and communities in becoming more supportive of families. Their address can be found in the appendix under *Associations*.

The lack of support that is available to parents is unacceptable and it is harmful. Parents should be able to take care of their own babies and small children. Too many people have been robbed of this choice. But here you are with your newborn and you must deal with your particular situation the best you can given your circumstances today.

Many of you will automatically feel you have to use daycare. But re-evaluate your choices before you settle on daycare as your only option, because a good substitute parent is difficult to find. One of you staying home for the first 6 to 12 months with your baby is a tall order, but the first year is critical. My husband and I decided to go into debt in order to allow me to stay home with our first child. This would not work for everyone, but it was worth it for us. There are ways to arrange to have one parent home, but first you have to assume it *could* be an option.

If you have to work, explore the possibility of performing your regular job, or career, at home. Telecommuting—working at your home instead of going into the office—is becoming more popular and there are a number of companies utilizing this option. Job sharing and flextime are also possibilities. These allow you to continue in your current position, but allow you to work your job around your baby's schedule instead of the other way around. If these options aren't available, consider performing a service you can do while having your baby with you, such as: taking care of one or two other children in your home, employment in phone sales, starting a typing service or some other home business, taking care of a housebound person, running errands for people, sewing, cooking, gardening or selling hand-crafted items.

Until your baby is mobile she will be quite content being carried in a baby sling, sleeping in a portable carrier, and watching you work. Later on you will want to work during baby's nap time and in shorter spurts. You might think about hiring a young mother's helper to watch and play with your baby while you work. I used to pay some responsible home-schooled girls to watch my kids while I worked upstairs. I was there for questions, emergencies and serious crying bouts, but did not have to entertain, get snacks, and watch them. The price was reasonable and my kids enjoyed it. Another option is for you and your mate to work different schedules so one or the other of you is at home most of the time. This may be hard on your relationship because you won't be seeing as much of each other, but it will last a relatively short time.

You can also try cutting down on expenses to reduce your financial needs. To do this with less frustration, you might want to watch less television, since commercials are meant to manipulate you into buying more. When you see commercials for seductively exciting adult toys, remind yourself that none of them are going to make you feel as good as having a healthy child. In addition, when you go to the store, bring a list and don't buy ANYTHING else. No impulse buying. Again, it is enticing seeing all the things that momentarily excite you, but the feeling won't last. Keep asking yourself, when it comes down to either buying things or having more time with your baby, which is ultimately more important? The less money you need to earn, the more time you'll have with your child, and isn't that why you wanted to have a child—to be with her?

One word of caution to mothers who know they will be returning to work right away: sometimes you might try to protect yourself from feeling the loss of your baby by never fully bonding with him or her. This self protection is understandable but harmful. If there is a decision to be made as to who might suffer, you, the adult, are much better equipped to cope with loss than your baby. It is better for you to struggle with your grief than avoid your infant. Don't sacrifice one bit of bonding now in order to protect yourself from missing your baby in the future. Check the appendix for resources that address work, jobs and related issues.

Daycare

The debate about the effects of daycare is extremely political and any statements on the subject are easily misconstrued one way or the other. After all, millions of children are in daycare. How can we critically discuss it without having twice that number of parents in a panic? My only agenda is to present what is optimal for fostering the healthy development of children and the best ways of implementing the best care possible.

Generalizations are impossible to avoid and obviously can not prescribe what is best for every child or every family. Most parents are stuck between a rock and a hard place and solutions are not necessarily ideal. I have only the greatest respect and compassion for parents and recognize that each of us is doing the best he or she can. Like it or not, we can't always live up to our or anybody else's expectations. That is a reality every parent faces every day. Many parents don't feel right about putting their infant in daycare, but they simply don't have any other choice. They have to believe daycare isn't harmful, otherwise they would be fraught with worry.

Nevertheless, we can't disregard what we know about what a baby needs for healthy development. The truth is that sometimes daycare is detrimental to your child and sometimes it isn't. If you choose your provider wisely, educate her, and minimize the number of hours you are away, and maintain a secure bond with your child, your chances are better that your baby won't be compromised.

Objective discussions about substitute care among child development experts and researchers in the field are difficult to achieve. Not only is the subject highly political but it is almost impossible to structure a study that isn't flawed. The number of variables that can enter the picture make drawing meaningful conclusions extremely difficult. What is the quality of childcare being studied? How does that compare to what most parents have access to or predominantly use? Isn't the quality of childcare as individual as the childcare providers themselves? What about the variety of home situations of the children being studied: how varied are they? How different are the stresses on the full-time working single parent and on two working parents from stresses on the family with one parent at home full-time? How are the behaviors of babies and children under three being evaluated? What about long-term effects that may not show up right away? All of these issues play heavily on what kind of results are obtained in any one study. In general, meaningful results are obtained from many research projects coming up with similar findings.

Recently, a long-term study conducted by The National Institute of Child Health and Human Development (NICHD) was released that raised a lot of commotion. The major claim made was that daycare in and of itself does not interfere with the mother-child bond and may actually improve cognitive development. But the majority of the media misrepresented the findings and only highlighted the aspects that reflected the popular hope that daycare is benign.

In fact the results demonstrated that:

- If a child has an insensitive mother, then the quality of the childcare and the quantity of time spent there matters a great deal.

- Children with insensitive mothers who are placed with an insensitive caretaker are often insecurely attached.

- A sensitive mother is the most important factor in predicting a child's secure attachment.

- If a mother is insensitive to her child's needs, it is even more important that she not have her child in daycare for more than 10 hours a week.

- High quality daycare does not compensate for poor care at home.

- The quality of interaction between caretaker and child is related to higher scores in language and cognition. However, only one third of providers have training in child development.

In addition, the media neglected to report how combinations of risk factors produce a higher incidence of insecure attachments. For instance, an insensitive mother's child who attended low quality childcare for more than 10 hours a week during the first year had a higher incidence of insecurity than either factor alone would indicate.

Another omission by the media was the general question of how the NICHD study could come up with numbers that were so contrary to the myriad of other studies that have been conducted on the effects of daycare. Many important studies have shown that:

- More than 20 hours a week of daycare in the first 12 months produces an insecurely attached child more than half the time. (Belsky and Rovine, 1988)

- Security of attachment is more likely in home-raised children.

The NICHD study was considered, by some, to be flawed because it improperly applied the Strange Situation (See "What Babies Need") as a diagnostic tool. Instead of studying the children at 12 and 18 months as the Strange Situation studies were designed to do, the children were evaluated at 15 months. Also, one has to wonder about the objectivity of a study about childcare that employs working mothers and fathers as researchers. Is it quite possible that their interpretations were biased in favor of daycare? In addition, the study was designed to look at long-term effects of daycare. It is too early to draw meaningful conclusions.

Babies cry so often, it's difficult imagining that their misery is really as serious as it sounds. We don't believe that a child's pleas not to be left in a stranger's arms are really such a big deal. After all, we know our baby is safe, but baby's genetic coding doesn't know it. We forget that each cry is made in the place of carefully selected words. Their screams, and other vocalizations, are the only ways they have to inform you of the instruction manual nature has provided in their DNA. We've been told not to believe that baby's fussing represents the kind of distress that will have any lasting consequence. However, studies have shown that children can appear to be at ease and yet their heart rate, blood pressure, and rate of respiration will reveal that they are extremely upset. Separation anxiety is not to be taken lightly.

Babies learn to expect the sensations and sequences of behavior that they are *repeatedly* exposed to. Specific patterns of behavior are coupled with a kind of sensory memory that tells babies how to adapt to their present circumstances. Whatever infants are consistently exposed to is what they will learn to imitate and respond to. The experiences of their day will become their models, and the architects of their brain.

Having said all this, the fact remains that almost half of all children will be in childcare for their first year. That doesn't make any of you who will use daycare bad parents and it certainly doesn't mean you should beat yourself up with guilt. Guilt will only make your situation more difficult. Focus on making your particular situation work as well as possible. Make sure you find the right childcare provider for your child.

It would be ideal if your childcare provider were a family member whom you trust. The more a person cares about your baby the better the quality of care that will be given. But whoever it is that takes care of your child, he or she should be practicing attachment parenting. Your child should securely bond with his or her childcare provider. More than likely you will need to instruct the provider on how to do this. For instance, you could give them this book to read. Even family members may need to be specifically told of your expectations. Emphasize that you want your child promptly picked up when she cries, to be held until she stops, and to be carried often. Tell them to talk to your child and have meaningful interactions with her (eye contact, face to face dialogues, etc.). And inform them of the possible discomforts your child might encounter, such as tendencies to be hot, gassy, hungry, easily over-stimulated, bored, etc.

Often, childcare providers spend more time with your child than you do so the quality of care is critical. It is vital that they show the same delight, concern, and consistency that a parent would.

If there is no family member to help out, then the next best situation would be for someone to come to your home. That way your baby doesn't have to adjust to new surroundings and get used to all new sights and smells. Separating from you is already a lot to deal with. Changing environments only adds to the stress. However, this option is more expensive than group daycare, so you might consider sharing this arrangement with another mother.

The third best choice for daycare would be to find a mom who is caring for just one or two other kids in her own home. Women who are currently parenting their own young children naturally tend to be more responsive and hopefully their homes will be fully baby-proofed. The one drawback about this arrangement of relying on someone in her home is that there are no other adults around to be held accountable. You can't be sure what is going on. In addition, this more private daycare arrangement is not as carefully regulated as licensed facilities, if at all. You will have to make sure that the environment is safe and the mom competent.

If, the first time you walk in, you find that the house is dirty and the TV is on, turn around and walk out the door. If your first impressions are favorable, talk to the other mothers who use her service and ask their impressions. Ask to look all around the house and yard for signs of hazards. Are electrical plugs covered, cabinets locked, toxic or dangerous substances put away? Are the toys clean and in good shape? Does the mom seem relaxed or frazzled? How does she respond to crying babies? Try to evaluate the health of her own child. This can often clue you in as to what kind of care your own child will be receiving.

If none of the above situations can be arranged, look for a small childcare center. Find out what their philosophy is before you tell them yours. Try to get a sense of how much they care about the kids versus how much it is simply another business. When you walk in, does it feel chaotic? Do the other children look happy? Is there a TV on all the time? Are the workers playing with the children or watching them play? Find out how many babies are in their care, whether or not they are licensed, trained in CPR, and what their guidelines are for calling you about your child, especially if she gets hurt or becomes ill.

Least desirable would be a large commercial childcare center that has as many as 20 to 30 kids. Not only is your child exposed to that many more illnesses, but it is usually hard to find one that provides good care for babies. If this is your only choice it is still better than leaving your baby unattended. NEVER LEAVE YOUR BABY ALL ALONE.

When choosing any childcare provider you should check the following:

- Does the provider have too many children? A chaotic, stressful environment will not be good for your baby. There should be a ratio of no less than one adult to every two or three babies, or one adult per six kids older than three. Older children require less attention and ratios can be higher, but babies simply need too much attention for caretakers to be stretched beyond a ratio of three to one.

- Get a feel for how caretakers will handle your child. Ask them about their previous experience. Definitely check references by calling past or present moms whose children they have cared for. Check with the Better Business Bureau to see if any complaints have been lodged against the provider. Make sure their license is current. In the case of hiring a single individual, check to see if he or she has a police record. This is not being paranoid, just being cautious. I encourage you to do a thorough background check of anyone who takes care of your child. Too many parents have been tragically fooled by what appeared to be well meaning, even loving caretakers. You can't always believe what you are told. The stakes are too high for you to not feel completely confident in whomever is dealing with your child. Nannies or babysitters don't have anyone else around to witness incidents of abuse, and children often are unable to tell you, even if they are old enough to talk. Abused children can still love their abuser, which can further confuse you. Do not ignore multiple incidents of illness or accidents and always pay attention to your intuition.

• Ask caretakers how they would respond in an emergency. Would they (or you, for that matter) know what to do if your child were choking or stopped breathing? Do they know CPR? Is there an available person with a car to take them to a hospital if necessary? What kinds of behaviors would prompt them to get in touch with you? How badly hurt does the child need to be, or how sick?

• What is their caretaking philosophy? Are they willing to carry or wear your baby often? How will they handle your child if he cries? Will they pick him up, talk to him, and tune into what might be wrong? How will they put him down for a nap? Will he cry until he goes to sleep, or be given help settling down? Will they feed him when he's hungry or according to a schedule? Do they have the TV on a lot and do they rely on swings and rockers to soothe a baby? In general, do you get the feeling they enjoy babies or are they *managing* the infants' behavior? Are they quieting them or responding to their needs?

- Is the environment clean and safe? All measures of safety should be used including proper food handling and storage practices. Do caretakers wash their hands between diaper changes? Are there toys that babies could choke on or which could hurt them? Are the toys broken or dirty? Are the floors, and kitchen, and bathroom clean (even if they are messy)? What will the meal arrangement be? Will they supply lunch or snacks and, if so, what kind of food and drink will be provided? What are the restrictions around allowing sick children to attend? Even though you may be inconvenienced at times by a strict policy, you won't want your baby exposed to unnecessary illnesses.

- Is the daycare center likely to still be in business next year? Try not to change childcare providers if you can help it. Remember that anyone who is your child's primary caretaker will hopefully develop a bond with your child.

To answer the above questions will require you to spend some time observing potential childcare providers. If any of them objects to this I would find someone else. When you do decide on a provider, stay with your child for several days while he gets used to the new people. If your baby is under three months old you may not immediately see that his separating from you is upsetting, but be assured that it is. Attachment behavior isn't readily apparent until 6 to 9 months but babies experience separation nonetheless.

Even if you think you have found a jewel of a caretaker, you should still be on the lookout for any worrisome changes in your child's behavior. If your child starts waking up in fright, resists going to bed, stops eating well, becomes withdrawn, anxious, clingy, or easily startled, be sure to take note. Follow up on your concerns by discussing them with your child's caretakers. Ask them what they see and observe. If they are totally unaware of what you are noticing, I would be wary. Why aren't they as tuned into your child as you are? Some of these changes in your child's behavior can occur naturally and are not necessarily caused by poor childcare, but you can't assume this is the case.

A baby will go through various stages, but she doesn't usually go from being a happy, outgoing child, to a sullen, withdrawn one in a matter of weeks. The possibility that your child is being abused is something you have to consider, even if you find it unthinkable. Other changes that should cause you even greater concern would be: the signs of insecure attachment, such as a lack of eye contact and avoiding or resisting you upon your return; persistent resistance to being left with the childcare provider; suspicious bruising; problems with urination; or unusual irritation around the genitals.

If you have any question, at any time, as to the safety and well-being of your child, act first, ask questions later. Do not leave your child with anyone with whom you are uncomfortable. If your child is being abused or neglected, she will start showing symptoms. Even if your child is going through a normal phase of not eating or sleeping well, crying more easily or feeling clingy, you should still be able to feel a bond with your child and believe that, overall, your child is doing well.

Resources that address concerns about daycare can be found in the appendix.

PART THREE

Disconnected

Common Problems

There are many reasons why parents may have problems bonding with and staying bonded to their babies, but they usually fall into a few basic categories. The parents are focused on themselves instead of the baby because they are in pain, depressed, anxious, insecure, or are having problems with money, time, jobs, relationships, addictions, etc. Or they may feel unable to focus on their baby because the baby is sick, deformed, handicapped, difficult, unattractive, or too demanding. Or they are following someone's bad advice and it's interfering with bonding. In addition, medical problems can be an issue, life circumstances may interfere, or the personality differences between parent and child can make it hard for the two to connect.

Sometimes parents who are aware of a problem between themselves and their child feel as if circumstances are out of their control. Other parents may not be able to face that they don't feel bonded with their child and try to ignore or deny their problem. Often parents don't see the disconnection coming. Events unfold gradually, other priorities slowly win their attention. Feelings envelop them in a world separate from their child.

It won't be good for you or your child to grow up feeling disconnected. When you are bonded you don't merely love each other, you know each other, enjoy each other. You share. Loving is a feeling, sharing is an interaction. Being part of each other's lives requires give and take, sensitivity to one another's needs, and a willingness to negotiate with care instead of power. Sharing your baby's world and having him or her share in yours is what sets the stage for your child to learn some of the most important life skills he or she will need to know.

Reconnecting with your baby may require you to be more tenacious initially, but forming a secure bond with your child is always achievable, even with autistic or emotionally handicapped children. Physical or biological handicaps can hinder the process but rarely inhibit it altogether. Even the most autistic children who, as a rule, live most of their lives in a state of retreat, demonstrate strong bonds with their caretakers. So important and so strong is a baby's drive to attach herself to a trusted and loving caretaker that almost nothing can destroy the desire for that connection, at least until children become older.

Sometimes the most difficult problems to tackle are those that interfere with bonding from the start. Here are a few examples of obstacles that some women face right after the birth.

- Some women have a traumatic labor and delivery and don't fully recuperate afterwards, emotionally and/or physically. They may have felt unprepared for the intensity of labor and birth and they feel shell-shocked, disappointed in themselves, and as a result, withdrawn.

- They may feel a little afraid about becoming a parent and avoid their baby to avoid their fear.
- They are distracted by their pain and exhaustion and are unable to focus much on their baby.
- Women who have cesarean deliveries, or who are given pain medication may spend less time bonding with their babies in the beginning. This gets the bonding process off on the wrong foot.
- Women who stay in the hospital and who don't have their babies rooming with them may not have enough opportunities to bond. This pattern may continue after they both come home.
- Initially, if the baby looks physically unappealing, the mother may feel disappointed and not want to bond with her unattractive infant. (Babies can look almost deformed right after the birth from being squeezed through the birth canal. They also are often blotchy and scrawny looking. All this will go away in time.)
- Mothers are afraid of accidentally hurting their fragile newborn and so avoid holding the child. They don't trust themselves as mothers.

If you get off to a rocky start, difficulties in the bonding process can snowball. You want to intervene as early as possible and get back on the right track. The first thing you want to do is to examine and understand what is keeping you from feeling bonded with your child. The following pages contain an in-depth look at situations that can interfere with a secure attachment to your child.

Feeling Disappointed

Most parents have some kind of expectation about what their baby is going to be like and how becoming a parent is going to feel. When those expectations aren't fulfilled, which they never can be completely, sometimes parents feel let down. If the expectation was great, the fall to reality can be far. If you don't love your baby right away, if parenting him or her is more difficult than you thought it would be, these feelings can interfere with bonding with your baby. Becoming aware of how you feel is half the battle. Admit that you feel disappointed. It's okay not to feel perfectly in tune and ecstatic; sometimes it takes a while to make the adjustment. If you recognize what's going on you can start addressing your feelings and do something about them. If you ignore these feelings, they may not "just go away" and they will hamper your ability to fully engage with your baby. Increase bonding activities, especially skin to skin contact, breastfeeding, and eye contact. These activities activate the release of oxytocin, a hormone that helps to cement feelings of attachment for the mother.

Busy

Imagine you are your baby. You've been in a crib or a playpen most of the day with a few musical toys and rattles. It's the afternoon and you've just had it. Your diaper is wet and cold next to your skin and you're bored, and hungry too. So you start crying. Eventually someone comes and puts you in a clean diaper but she doesn't really talk to you. There are words but no meaning to them, no eye contact, no interaction. Then you are put back in your crib. Alone and insecure, you cry again, and the caretaker props you up with a bottle in your mouth. This doesn't do the trick for long though and you fuss some more. But no one comes. You fuss louder, harder; finally someone shows up and puts a pacifier in your mouth. It works for a time, but you're still unhappy because you're not getting what you need. This time the caretaker puts you in the swing, which is entertaining, but ultimately it doesn't satisfy your need to be close to someone and to learn about the world. After a time, you give up and just sit there. (While the caretaker is thinking, "Oh good, she's finally quiet.") Baby may learn to stop asking for what she needs and caretakers won't realize their baby is not feeling securely bonded.

How common is a scene like this one? To some degree, all too common. Everyone is so busy these days, from parents to day-care workers. It is not unusual to see babies being treated as "things" to be quieted. They get their diapers changed and bottles delivered, they get mechanically rocked and bounced in swings and seats, and they are given lots of temporary substitute soothers. But they're not *with* anyone. They're not part of conversations and interactions. They're not being held and carried and kept close to that trusted someone who makes them feel secure. Instead they are given distractions like wind-up mobiles that never quite fill the need. They go from one gadget to another, distracted but not engaged. They're quieted but not because they've been given what THEY need. When a baby cries out she is talking to you. She has a message that she needs you to tune into. When we treat babies as things to be quieted, we start losing our bond with them.

The caretaker in this example is not really neglecting the baby; after all the infant is being changed and fed and responded to some of the time. Isn't this good enough? Isn't it going a little overboard to give more than this? No. This is not a minor point. This baby is ingesting models of the world that are going to be part of how she feels about and interprets life. She's not learning about how to listen to others—how to respond to and trust others. She isn't being stimulated to learn language and meaning. She isn't being supported in having more calm mental alertness, and she doesn't have touch and movement to stimulate a number of physiological and biological systems. It all adds up to being very significant. And the cure is so simple. If this baby were in a baby carrier, close to her parent or caretaker, talked to and interacted with, her development would be radically different, as would her feelings of security. Taking time to enjoy your child is an important bonding activity. Being too busy is not good for you and it is not going to be good for your baby.

Premature and Hospitalized Babies

When you are not with your baby in the first few days or weeks after the birth, bonding can be hindered. A baby who hasn't been responded to regularly may not be very good at calling to have her needs met, and even when her needs are attended to, a premature or sick baby may still have a difficult time settling down. By the time babies leave the hospital, they may have learned to be more passive in their fussing and other signaling cues. Or the very opposite may be true. They may have learned to be tenacious in their demands and may often be in a state of agitation. In the hospital it is difficult for nurses to hold and tend to all the needs of the preemies and sick babies in their charge. These babies start out with inconsistent care and they may, initially, exhibit signs of insecure attachment.

The preemie and hospitalized baby will usually have more difficulty bonding because they have endured a lot of discomfort and insecurity. By the time parents get their baby home, their child is sometimes several months old, but parents must deal with their baby as if she were still a newborn. Their baby will most likely lack the organization needed to deal well with upsets and strong sensations. She will need you to help her recover and feel soothed. Sensations will feel chaotic and disturbing for the stressed preemie. Many premature babies continue to be easily overstimulated for months. You may need to let your baby stay in the kangaroo pouch mode for as long as 9 to 12 months. Don't be surprised if she asks to be carried a lot. In addition, you will need to help your baby focus on your face and make eye contact. Getting a dialogue going may take more of an effort. You'll also need to provide for her security and stimulation even though your baby doesn't tell you when she needs it.

If your child is still in the hospital, hold and talk to her as much as possible. Studies have shown that your baby will leave the hospital sooner, grow faster, and be more intelligent the more she is held and touched.

Adoption

Many of the same issues exist concerning adopted children as they do in regards to hospitalized babies. The bonding process has been disrupted. If the baby is adopted right after birth, that disruption will be mild. If, however, many months have elapsed and care has been inadequate, your adopted child may already be quite distressed, or show signs of being insecurely attached.

In utero experiences are also very significant and can affect a baby's ability to bond. If the mother was very angry and resentful of her pregnancy, if she was emotionally or physically abused while pregnant, or abused drugs, the baby can be affected. In addition, if the baby, after birth, was neglected or abused, bonding will take longer and require you to be much more persistent in forming that connection. Babies or children who have lacked comfort at such a young age are at a high risk of acquiring an attachment disorder.

Colicky Babies

Colic is not well understood and sometimes it is difficult to diagnose. However, if a baby cries inconsolably three to four times a week, especially at the same time of the day or night, the pattern started when the baby was about a month old, and he is otherwise healthy, colic is usually cited as the cause. These crying sessions can last for hours and nothing you do may help. The good news is that colic rarely lasts longer than three months, and it is not a disease.

There are mixed opinions as to what causes colic and gas is only one of them, but it may be the only one you can treat successfully. Digestive disorders can cause your child to be in pain and you should try to eliminate this as a cause. If you are breast-feeding be aware of eating gassy, spicy, or acidic foods. My baby once cried for three days after I drank orange juice. My next breastfed baby couldn't digest the dairy products I was eating. Other digestion problems may be caused by a baby overeating or taking in too much air while feeding, both of which are common in bottlefed babies.

Even though you may be relieved to have determined that your child is having episodes of colic rather than expressing a serious medical condition, inconsolable crying can be extremely hard on parents, especially if the disturbance is in the middle of the night. It's so distressing to listen to your baby wail and not be able to help her. It is very important to get breaks from it. One couple I knew took turns every night being the one to tend to the baby while the free parent got as far from the noise as possible. He or she would sit outside, take a walk, get a cup of herbal tea, go to the library, or simply use ear plugs. Ear plugs may actually help both parents out. You still hear the crying, but it's muted.

When you are with your crying infant, remind yourself that she is not in a life threatening situation, and that all she needs is your calm and loving comfort. Sing to your baby, tell her stories, play music, walk into different rooms, and assure her it will be all right. Carrying your infant in a semi-erect position so that any digestive disturbance won't be aggravated can also help. Some parents use a hot water bottle covered with a towel, or a heating pad on a low setting, placed under their baby's tummy as a calming device. You'll need to experiment to see what your baby may respond to. The thing you don't want to do is leave your baby alone to deal with it herself—unless that is what she clearly indicates she wants. Some babies don't want even the stimulation of being held, but that is rare. Even then they will want verbal reassurance.

Bonding may be challenged because colic is so trying for both baby and parent. You may find yourself becoming resentful of your baby and exasperated with your inability to help her. Eventually you stop trying to help. You are drained by these regular episodes of crying and you have little left to give the rest of the time. (Reread the section on getting support.) For many years to come your child is going to cry and you won't always be able to take away the pain. Offering comfort and support to your baby can be even more important at times like these. Don't give up in your efforts to be responsive. Your baby really doesn't mean to put you through so much turmoil. Remember: This too shall pass.

Chronic Pain

Chronic ear infections and other painful diagnosed or undiagnosed problems can interfere with bonding. Pain is distracting. Babies in severe pain can't focus on connecting with anybody because they are preoccupied with their discomfort. They are unable to experience and ingest the models of care to which they are exposed.

Chronic pain can also interfere with normal brain development. When pain centers are continuously stimulated, neural receptors in that part of the brain grow more connections. This can cause a baby to become hypersensitive and easily aroused. This also makes it difficult for the caretaker to like the child, because so often he is unhappy and fussy.

In addition, the experience of constant discomfort can cause babies to learn to tune out their bodies and begin to form patterns of disconnecting from their own feelings—a dangerous trend. These babies are at high risk of becoming insecurely attached if much isn't done to soothe and comfort them.

Fussy Babies

Fussy babies may be indicating that they are *already* feeling insecurely attached. If there are too many occasions that they have been made to wonder "Will help come this time or not?", if they have been left in their discomfort and fear too often, they will be in a state of agitation more often than not. They will learn to employ more insistent ways of communicating their feelings. Now every time baby needs help he is prepared to exhibit tremendous urgency. Instead of having a time of respite in between urges, the inconsistently responded to child will linger in states of anticipation. This constant agitation makes it harder for baby to get comfortable and relax, and pretty soon even minor discomforts become unbearable. Before you know it, your baby is fussy more times than not. This is not a very engaging state for the caretakers (parent or childcare provider) and may cause them to be less engaged.

An insecure attachment is not the only cause of fussiness. Again, it is important to note the difference between insecurely attached babies who act fussy and "high need" babies, who are expressing their personality or temperament. Babies who are fussy but securely attached are able to 1) make eye contact, 2) accept comforting without routinely avoiding or resisting it, 3) explore the environment with curiosity and interest and 4) regularly focus on the caretaker and participate in reciprocal exchanges or "dialogues". They may need to be held and responded to often; they may even be squirmy and sensitive to change, but they also exhibit the signs of a secure attachment.

Babies who are naturally high strung or sensitive may just be displaying how bright and aware they are. They may need more holding, feeding, comforting, and soothing, and often can't get comfortable very easily, but they are not bad babies. They don't mean to demand more, it's just who they are. Today your baby is fussy because she is hyper-aware and over-stimulated. Tomorrow that awareness may help her to become a brain surgeon or find the secret to world peace. Right now you may need to do more rocking and holding, but in the long run, your baby will benefit from your caring about her discomfort.

Whatever you do, try not to resent or turn away from a high need child. Your persistent patience and care will pay off in the long run.

Feeling Rejected By Your Baby

Your baby doesn't hold opinions; she only has reactions. All she knows is whether or not her needs are being met: her need to be loved, to feel safe and comfortable, and to interact with the world. If you feel like your baby doesn't love you, understand that she is incapable of sizing you up as a person and rejecting you based on how you rate. Maybe she's in pain or is having difficulty with seeing and hearing. She may be easily overstimulated. If you feel that your baby is unresponsive to you, step up bonding activities. If the symptoms continue, it may indicate that something else is wrong. When in doubt, ask your pediatrician.

Inadequate Daycare

Whoever spends a great deal of time with your baby is going to be as important as a parent to some degree. Babies need to feel securely attached to that person and receive the kind of care that promotes bonding. Review the chapter on daycare.

Bad Fit

The personality of the baby and parents are a bad match. For instance, the baby may be quiet and passive and the parents equally so. The baby doesn't ask for much and the parents don't offer a lot. As a result this baby may not get some essential stimulation and care. Or what if the baby is sensitive and the parents boisterous; or the baby is very active and demanding and the parents are quiet and withholding. There are a number of combinations that require parents to make a concerted effort in forming a secure bond with their child. Parents need to be aware of their child's unique temperament and modify their own behavior in order to accommodate their child's needs.

The Past Intrudes

You may be feeling unhappy in your new role as parent because your past has come back to haunt you. Unresolved or unhappy childhood memories have crept into your thoughts and feelings. The parent-child relationship has more negative associations than positive ones and you are anxious or depressed as a result. This can occur even without you being conscious of any particular memories. It may be a good time to get some counseling. These negative feelings can seriously impair your ability to bond with your baby.

♥ Postpartum Depression

Most new moms experience "the blues" after their baby is born and for very good reasons. After all, your body just went through a major ordeal, your whole life changed dramatically, and you're probably not getting enough sleep. In addition, you are going through hormonal adjustments that are no small matter. But the baby blues are a state you can live with and within a few weeks they go away. True postpartum depression is much more disruptive and affects the quality of your life. All mothers with newborns are tired, but they can still get out of bed to shower and make breakfast. If you are seriously depressed, you don't want to get out of bed. You undereat or overeat. You often feel anxious and unable to get to sleep. You may cry a lot, feel very irritable, or even confused. This kind of depression often does not just go away and needs to be attended to.

One reason you may be depressed is because you didn't have the opportunity or ability to bond with your baby in the first few weeks after the birth. Bonding is not only important for your baby but works to regulate important hormone levels in you. Pregnancy and childbirth constitute a physiological marathon that requires the body to alter its normal functioning by manufacturing increased levels of certain chemicals. The mechanisms that re-balance the body are contained, in part, in activities like breastfeeding and having skin contact with your baby. Attachment behaviors can help ease you out of your hormonal hurricane. Oxytocin and prolactin, which are released when you're nursing, are only two of the chemicals that work to stabilize you. When you have skin contact with your baby, the changes in your body chemistry are measurable. Cooperating with the designs of nature again proves to be beneficial. What a perfect design—being close to baby is good for your depression!

Another reason your depression may be severe is because of what is going on in your life. If you are in turmoil about your relationship, money, job, family, or health, or if you are fretting, stressed and preoccupied with external events, then parenting is going to be the last straw that sends you to bed. Too much is too much. Excessive demands can leave you wrung out and exhausted. If you go into overload, your body is going to shut down to some extent, and become depressed.

Put anything and everything that causes you anxiety aside for now. Stop thinking about anything else but your baby. This is not the time to solve life's problems. Almost everything can wait until you have a chance to recuperate and settle into your new life.

You may become angry at your mate during this time which can suddenly isolate you and add to your stress. Try to realize that your perspective may be quite altered right now. You naturally feel overwhelmed, physically and emotionally. Becoming a new parent is a lot to deal with. Anxiety and irritability are a logical outcome but you don't have to let them take you over. What you need is to ask for support, and offer understanding to your partner, who is also overwhelmed. Your partner is not your enemy. Instead of blaming your mate for not meeting certain expectations, state how *you* are feeling. Work together. Come up with a plan for minimizing your obligations and getting more support for the family.

Put aside as many chores and obligations as you can right now. If you can afford it, hire a house cleaner to come in once a week for the first month. Ask a good friend or family member to do your laundry or shopping. Use paper plates for a few weeks, buy healthy frozen food, put aside unnecessary errands, and forget about getting much of anything done other than enjoying your baby and pampering yourself.

You can also get stressed out from doing too little for yourself. If you never get out, feel isolated, alone and unsupported, parenting can feel like a black hole. Just because you have this new life to tend to doesn't mean you stop taking care of your own. Enjoy taking warm baths (which can be enjoyable to do with your baby as well), listen to music you like, exchange massages with your mate (or spring for a professional massage). Also, you can and should get out with your baby sometimes. Put him in a baby carrier and go for a walk. Go visit a friend or go out to lunch. Infancy is an easier time to cart your baby around than when he is older. He is light and sleeps a lot (babies can get used to sleeping just about anywhere, although some easily overstimulated babies might initially need more quiet or fewer distractions).

Sometimes it's difficult to know whether your depression is being caused by external events, inner conflicts, or chemical imbalances. Sometimes you can feel sad and think your mate or money worry is the cause, when in fact you are being triggered into depressive thinking by imbalances in your body. If you don't feel capable of telling yourself, "Things aren't so bad; they will improve; this is just a difficult period," then you need to see a professional. Don't deny your true feelings.

Great strides have been made in the area of medication and many are getting relief that ten years ago wouldn't have been possible. Even certain herbs such as St. John's Wort have been proven to be effective, and more doctors are recommending it to treat depression. It is still unclear whether depression causes chemical imbalances or that the imbalances cause the depression or that the cause is both working in tandem. Either way, medication used in conjunction with therapy can be very effective.

Other possible chemical imbalances that can cause depression are thyroid disorders. There are several types and you would need to be diagnosed by a physician. I had a thyroid condition that was brought on by high levels of stress (including the physically challenging experiences of pregnancy and childbirth), but which was undiagnosed for years. I experienced the symptoms of a thyroid condition. But my blood test for thyroid disorders always came back normal. My condition was later identified as low T3.

If you have unexplained weight gain, digestive disorders, fatigue, forgetfulness, inability to concentrate, lethargy, and dry skin, to name just some of the possible symptoms, you may have a dysfunctional thyroid. Check with your doctor. If you notice that you also have low body temperature (check it several times a day) you may want to get more information about low T3 by calling the Wilson Foundation. The number is: 1-800-621-7006.

Depression is a serious problem and one that will not go unnoticed by your child. Studies have shown that babies are deeply disturbed if they experience a lack of expression on their mother's faces. In the "flat face" studies babies as young as three months would become visibly upset if their mothers looked at them with no emotion on their faces at all, just a flat affect. Depressed mothers are at high risk of having babies with attachment disorders.

More helpful hints for transforming depression, or learning to take care of yourself again:

- Remember to schedule breaks for yourself. Getting in some alone time is essential. Going to the magazine room at the library was one of my favorite escapes.

- Exercise releases stress. You can hike, walk, bike, jog, or workout to a video with your baby on your back, in tow, or nearby.

- Do something different once a month—a bike ride, racquet ball. Go swimming at the municipal pool, go to a lecture, a play, a class.

- With your mate or other parents, take turns giving each other a break.

- Ask a friend over for a potluck. Play a game like charades or cards.

- Sometimes just a half hour in the evening having a cup of tea and reading a magazine or book by yourself— uninterrupted—can make you feel human again. Take turns with your mate, or another mother.

- Pamper yourself. Do something that feels rewarding without being self-destructive or self-defeating.

- Play music you enjoy. Or experiment with listening to something you don't normally play. Music can quickly change your mood.

- Notice what is right before your eyes—life. Sometimes

it's intense and difficult; other times it is pure splendor.

- Every day, give at least as much attention to all that is right in your life as you do to all that is wrong. Gratitude can be a powerful healer.

If you are still not enjoying your baby, reread the section on bonding. But if you continue to feel depressed or anxious, if you're crying a lot, feeling out of control, if you're not taking care of the basics like washing, dressing, or eating, or if you are not sleeping well, then make sure you call your doctor or a counselor.

Consequences of an Insecure Attachment

EVERY DAY, in the United States, an estimated:

- 3-4 children will die due to abuse (an increase of 48% since 1985)
- 3-4 people will be killed by a child under 18 years old
- 15 children will die from guns
- 27 children will die from poverty
- 2,350 children can be found in adult jails
- 2,699 children will be born into poverty
- 8,189 children will be reported abused or neglected
- 135,000 children will bring guns to school

  (Reported by the Children's Defense Fund)

It is obvious our children are not fairing well. And, not surprisingly, they are maturing into adults who aren't doing well either—8 to 20 million people are experiencing the effects of depression, countless numbers suffer from addictions, and an appalling number are resolving conflicts using violence.

The incidence of children who kill, spousal abuse, crimes of passion, teen pregnancies and suicides, and antisocial personality disorders have increased at alarming rates in the last half of this century. These incidences constitute trends and will continue to get worse unless something is done. Statistics such as these should be frightening us out of our wits.

The web of causal factors is intricate and complex. Certainly, the lack of government leadership and support from the business community are primary reasons we're in so much trouble. From these emerge the specific villains of poverty, loss of community, lack of support for working parents, the shaping of our values by the media, the decline of philanthropic contributions and volunteering, and unhealthy life style practices.

The combination of years of parenting advice, which advocated less responsive care, and the common but unacceptable stress most parents face have made for a dangerous environment for our emerging children. Then, when a damaged child becomes a damaged adult who has a child, chances are good that the dysfunctional behavior will be handed down. Unfortunately, a large portion of our society has experienced some kind of dysfunctional parenting. There are now many who have had to build their lives on insecurity, pervasive anxiety, and depression. They have to struggle with their natural inclination to avoid intimacy and mistrust in their relationships. They have to fight against feelings of shame, low self-esteem and emptiness, and all this while parenting a child. The greatest obstacle to being an effective parent is never having been securely bonded as a child.

The securely attached infant learns he can effectively get his needs met. He expects to be successful. This expectation sets a chain reaction into motion that more likely than not will lead to a successful life later on. Satisfied needs represent a baby's successes, dissatisfied ones their failures. Without mostly triumphs, a baby may develop a poor self image and stop trying to get many of the experiences he needs in order to develop curiosity, creativity, empathy and cooperation. An album of memories with a record of necessities satisfied and frustrations resolved won't be there for baby to draw from in the future.

To give you an idea of what it might feel like to be a neglected baby imagine feeling afraid and physically uncomfortable, knowing there isn't a thing you can do but lie there and take it. You can't escape, distract yourself for very long, or get help. And you go through this every day, off and on for months, or even years. How would you cope? How would you deal with it if you didn't have the ability to talk to yourself and conjure up possible solutions, if you didn't know about time and so couldn't hope for a better tomorrow? What if you were unable to convince yourself that it really wasn't as bad as it seems? What would your options be then?

Besides falling asleep, one of your only alternatives would be to detach yourself from feeling anything at all—to divert your attention to anything other than your emotions, to separate—to not feel connected to yourself or anyone else. That fixes it. End of trauma. And that's what a baby's brain achieves when synapses are bathed in cortisol. The emotional centers are diminished, memory is affected and a baby is somewhat protected from chronic emotional pain. No feelings, no pain. But there is a cost.

If a child's brain is exposed to too much stress, if the models it's exposed to are violent and painful, that child will not know how to feel empathy and trust. If then the child learns how to protect himself from getting close to others and to get his needs met through manipulation, imagine the kind of life he would lead. If someone doesn't feel any connection to his or her own emotions, if he or she can't feel the pain of others it can spell disaster. If you can't feel the pain of others, then you can't operate with a conscience. If you have repressed rage and no conscience, anything is possible. The most horrific criminals we know of—serial killers, child molesters, and rapists—are often diagnosed as psychopaths, or those without a conscience. These individuals are not inherently evil but are suffering from the symptoms of an antisocial personality disorder that is strongly linked to a history of neglect and abuse as children. It's not difficult to see how the disturbances resulting from extremely insecure attachment histories could domino into producing emotionally disturbed individuals.

Patterns of behavior can snowball, picking up speed as they go. The problem is that we haven't been linking the string of behaviors that begin in infancy to the conduct disorders we see in adolescents or the more serious problems seen in teenagers. The baby who hasn't learned to trust and feel competent, the child who has grown up impulsive and angry, becomes increasingly more isolated as he grows older. The likelihood of being successful in jobs and relationships diminishes, adding to an already lengthy history of frustration. Anger slowly escalates, setting the stage for disaster. This person is spiraling downwards. His undeveloped social skills, mistrust of others, need to be in control, explosive or implosive (depressive) rage, impulsiveness, fears, and feelings of abandonment shape his life into becoming increasingly more dysfunctional. Frustration in employment and relationships can drive a person to deviate into addictive, self-destructive or dishonest behavior, or to become verbally, emotionally, sexually, or physically abusive to others. As the statistics show, scenarios such as these are becoming all too common.

The consequences of attachment disorders that persist into adolescence are more common than you might think. It is absolutely imperative that these children are correctly diagnosed early on and receive the proper treatment. The earlier this disorder is treated the better the prognosis. The following is a list of common symptoms of the older child with Reactive Attachment Disorder:

- Has problems forming and keeping friendships
- Is charming in the extreme along with being superficially sincere
- Avoids eye contact
- Has a history of escalating behavior problems at home and in school
- Consistently battles for control
- Has problems with impulse control
- Lacks cause and effect thinking
- Is manipulative and cunning
- Lies, cheats, and steals
- Uses drugs
- Engages in gang activity
- Bullies others
- Intentionally hurts self, animals or things
- Hoards food
- Is obsessed with fire, blood, and gore
- Engages in persistent nonsense questions and chattering

- Has abnormal speech patterns

- Has developmental lags

- Lacks a conscience

If we look at the kinds of problems we are having in our society, we will notice how many of them relate to the symptoms of unhealthy beginnings. Most of us are aghast at the growing population of people who are able to lie, cheat, steal, and/or take advantage of others. Consumer fraud and white collar crime, corrupt officials and deviant clergy, the amoral and unhealthy behavior that more and more people are exhibiting, and the extent to which it has become a normal part of our society should horrify us. But these aren't the only signs of how attachment disorders can grow into emotional chaos later in life.

Consider this list of some of the more common problems facing people today and how they relate to **what was missing** in their childhood.

- **Divorce and other relationship problems.** It seems like everyone is having a hard time getting along with someone. So far the majority of us don't shoot each other over parking spaces or stalk ex-lovers, but these are still disturbing signs of the times. Relationships with co-workers, spouses, love interests, our children, and neighbors are frequently strained and challenged. WHAT WAS MISSING: Being taught *by example* to respect the needs of others and a history of positive, satisfying interactions with a trusted someone.

- **Gang behavior.** Children who don't feel competent and valued become adults who want to feel potent and dominant. Those who have never felt securely attached look for ways to feel that they belong. WHAT WAS MISSING: Feeling connected to a family or a community. Low self-regard is the result of feeling emotionally abandoned and rejected, and from being unsuccessful at getting one's needs met.

• **Violent solutions to conflict.** Insecurity breeds fear and the need to be dominant. In addition, children who have been spanked learned that violence is acceptable. WHAT WAS MISSING: Consistent responses to baby's discomfort. He or she has been often left in tears and in a state of fear which programs the brain to be hypervigilant, angry, overactive, and impulsive. Also, parents who are abusive to each other and violent television programs, movies and video programs model aggressive behavior.

• **Addictions.** What could be more obvious proof of the psychic pain so many are in? No one starts taking drugs who already feels good. The exceptions are tobacco and alcohol whose dangers are hidden behind the advertising. WHAT WAS MISSING: Consistent relief from discomfort, grief, and frustration. Learning to cope required the formation of avoidance behaviors.

• **Thrill seeking** (having affairs, bungee jumping, etc.). An addiction to the endorphins that produce the rush of excitement. WHAT IS MISSING: Same elements as with other addictions. Added to this may be a history of boredom and a lack of stimulation—too many days spent in playpens.

• **Co-dependency.** This condition is the result of emotional starvation. Having been denied a secure bond with someone as a child, they feel hungry for love as an adult. They do whatever is necessary to win someone's love and approval. WHAT WAS MISSING: Sufficient love and security as a child.

• **Eating disorders.** Having been denied emotional nourishment, the compulsive overeater turns to food as a substitute. WHAT WAS MISSING: Consistent care, the lack of which produces low self-esteem and an absence of feelings of satisfaction. Anorexia nervosa, or self-imposed starvation, is a disorder very reminiscent of one from which babies who lack responsive care suffer—*failure to thrive.*

• **Suicide.** Self hate and hopelessness are the feelings that usually accompany those who take their own life. (Alcoholism and drug abuse are forms of slow suicide.) WHAT WAS MISSING: Secure attachments and a feeling that one is not alone. Also missing is a history of awareness that one can be helped, that the pain can be relieved. Sometimes the sadness is deeply embedded in neural pathways.

• **Depression.** Often described as anger turned inwards, but certainly can be caused by feeling abandoned and profound sadness and/or chemical imbalances. WHAT WAS MISSING: A life of repeated successes and satisfied needs. At the very least, sad and frustrated babies grow sad and frustrated brains.

• **Attention Deficit Disorder** (ADD), believed to be caused by impaired neurological functioning. Symptoms include poor impulse control, incessant chatter, inability to focus well, lack of cause and effect thinking, low threshold of frustration, and learning disabilities. These symptoms are very similar to Reactive Attachment Disorder. Not all, but probably at least some children diagnosed with ADD really have RAD. WHAT WAS MISSING: All aspects of a secure attachment.

• **Spousal and child abuse, rape, senseless killings, or, in other words, acts of rage gone haywire.** WHAT WAS MISSING: Healthy neurological development. The propensity towards violence is sometimes built into a baby's developing brain because he has been allowed to needlessly experience pain (physical or emotional) too often. People who "lose it" have been containing unmanageable discomfort. Additionally, abused and neglected children learn to treat others that way. Most importantly, violent television shows, movies, video games as well as a history of being hit make violence seem normal.

Not all insecurely attached children grow up to be emotional basket cases, but that does not discount the connection between attachment disorders and emotional problems later on. Some children will survive better than others because they have sturdier temperaments. They receive enough positive responses from somewhere to offset the damage done. A nurturing teacher, caring aunt, or friendly neighbor may be all a child needs to start him on the road to health. One significant episode of support can be enough to bring into play new mental constructs of hope. A hobby or healthy obsession can promote mastery and confidence in a person whose self-esteem was destroyed in childhood. Any one of these beneficial accidents can make the difference for a child who is by nature resilient. It can be enough to turn the tide for the child who is tenacious and determined, even if those traits originally developed for unhealthy reasons.

It can not be said that if a child is insecurely attached he will definitely become the next Ted Bundy. But the more severe the attachment disorder, the higher the probability he will manifest dysfunctional behavior as an adult. The combination of events and circumstances in a single life is too varied to accurately predict the future, but high probability is nothing to play Russian roulette with.

Too often we assume that babies can deal with feelings of abandonment, discomfort, and fear better than we can. We are gravely mistaken in concluding that babies simply bounce back from their ordeals. The flexibility that they do have is to adapt—whether that means to a healthy environment or an unhealthy one. If they adapt to an unhealthy environment, their personality development will follow suit.

Some scars don't heal. Our past does affect our future. Less severe forms of attachment disorders are less apt to turn into psychiatric disorders but they can still be detrimental to one's quality of life. And if symptoms of insecure attachment follow one into adulthood, stress can catapult everyday neurosis into more serious disorders or addictions.

Catching the problems early on is the key. In the first year, neurons are still being added and deleted. By the third year, specific neural pathways and behavior patterns have formed. By school age, conduct disorders may begin to manifest. Years of being punished and yelled at will have compounded already low self-esteem. But the brain is still malleable and can recover from the effects of a bad start.

However, by the time a child is twelve, much of his neurological development will have been completed and his behavior will be set. The brain will continue to grow new synapses, if asked to do so, well into old age, but there is a limit to the brain's flexibility as we get older.

Raising secure children is paramount if we are going to successfully alter today's statistics, but in the meantime, parents are required to make many sacrifices and give more than they should have to because vital support from community and government is lacking. It's up to all of us to shout louder for more to be done to ensure the healthy development of our children. More people need to join the ranks of Dr. T. Berry Brazelton and Dr. Penelope Leach, leading child development experts, in sounding the imperative to PUT CHILDREN FIRST.

The health of our children must take priority. It means that we must dare to speak the truth even if the solutions aren't yet obvious. We can not discover what is possible until we pledge our commitment to look for it. Now that we have so much in the way of hard science to support the principles of attachment theory, we can confidently embrace the child-rearing practices that promote secure attachments in children. We know what our goals must be.

If You Feel Like You Are Starting To Lose It

There were three million child abuse cases reported in 1994. Two-thirds of those were dismissed, but certainly many more cases were never reported. Nevertheless, one million is an astonishingly high number of children who are being permanently damaged every year. An alarming number of those children will go on to abuse their own children, and the number of abuse cases will continue to climb unless something is done.

That something starts with all parents committing, with all their hearts, to protecting their children and keeping them safe, even if it means having to face their own demons. We must stop the chain of abuse.

There are a number of reasons why parents act abusively. Usually it is because they themselves were mistreated. When abusive styles of parenting are learned, they seem normal. The parents don't see that what they're doing is harmful. They don't know another way to parent. They are emotionally damaged and don't feel they can control themselves. The anger they still carry for their abusers is taken out on their children.

The dynamics of the parenting relationship reawaken the associations of their own childhoods. When their children cry because they need more from their parents, it can trigger the parents into re-experiencing their own histories of frustrated tears. A reservoir of stored rage can suddenly become unleashed.

Often parents are in denial about their actions. Here is a sampling of some of the ways they justify their behavior:

I'm not really doing anything all that bad.

My child deserved it.

My child doesn't obey me unless I...(hit, yell, spank, etc.)

My child is different and needs tougher treatment.

Spanking worked for me when I was a child.

The things I say aren't mean.

I'm doing the best I can, (Which is always true—but that does not mean a parent is justified in abusing a child.)

What I'm doing is not abusive.

It won't happen again.

If you are a parent who feels he or she is losing it with a child, take a first step by examining how you feel. Maybe you feel very stressed out and overwhelmed. You can not cope, and your thoughts, feelings, and/or behavior seem out of your control. These feelings are very important to attend to. The answer is to do everything you can to minimize your load. If you can't find a solution get a friend or counselor to help you problem-solve.

Often when we feel overwhelmed, we feel cornered, boxed in. We can't envision a way out. Resist thinking that there is no way to change your life circumstance. That is never the case. The world will not end if you change your present course. Be open to suggestions, and remember, nothing will work until you are feeling better.

If you do get to the place where you are on the verge of hurting your child, walk into the next room and scream into a pillow. Call anyone and everyone you can: friends, agencies, churches. Try to find someone to come over and give you a break. If you can't do that, call a help line and at least talk to someone right away. In addition, find a way to calm yourself or re-direct your frustration. Take a hot shower, punch the bed, pray, put earplugs in if you can't stand hearing your child cry. Most importantly, DO NOT SHAKE YOUR BABY—this can cause serious brain damage and even death. Shaking your child will not make him behave better, it will only make him cry more.

You are frustrated and you want to get rid of those feelings. Do it in a way that doesn't hurt your child. If you can, hold your child close to your heart and tell yourself this won't last forever and that not hurting your baby is all that counts. Your child is innocent and never deserves to be hurt.

There are many parents who are without the basic necessities of life. It's no wonder child abuse statistics are so high. Poverty, inadequate prenatal and general health care, substandard child-care, housing, and diet, as well as a lack of community support doom families to a life of unmanageable stress. As a society we can't let these conditions continue. We each need to become active in our own ways to support the needs of children and families.

In the meantime, get support and ask for help. Do whatever you need to reduce your stress.

If you have been losing it with your child, you need to forgive yourself. Unless you feel better about who you are, it may be impossible for you to be more tolerant and forgiving of your child. However, do not allow yourself to think that losing control with your child is acceptable.

The Golden Rule

The principle contained in the golden rule, treat others the way you want them to treat you, is not only found in Christianity but has been at the foundation of many societies all over the world throughout time. Five hundred years before the Sermon on the Mount, Confucius wrote, "What you do not like when done to yourself do not do to others." This code has been prevalent in so many cultures because it is part of our evolutionary heritage. Our gene pool selected cooperation and helpful behavior as desirable traits because they enabled our ancestors to better survive and propagate. Ultimately, helping each other was more advantageous than not. Obtaining meaningful catches of food and hides was better done in teams. Joining forces to defeat a mutual enemy increased the potential for victory. Trading for services would double an individual's chances. As a result, those who were adept at enacting fair exchanges, and knew how to avoid exploiting and angering their neighbors were some of the ones who survived to pass on the characteristics that made them successful. Those traits included emotions that would guide them into prosperous rather than self-defeating behavior. Sympathy, compassion, gratitude and trust would lead to supportive and cooperative behaviors. Anger and moral indignation would stave off exploitation by potential adversaries, and guilt would guard one from trying to take advantage of others.

Maybe the reason why we developed attributes for altruistic behavior was ultimately motivated by the individual's selfish desire to live and multiply, but the end remains the same. At the core of our being, we are meant to live by the golden rule. And at the heart of this statement is the ultimate guide to parenting—**treat your children as you would want to be treated.**

By following this primary genetic instruction we are in harmony with the overall design that is meant to guide our behavior. By following the golden rule our feelings are in sync with how they were intended to operate. In this way the positive aspects of our emotions are brought out and we minimally employ the more aggressive side of our natures, which, if emphasized too much, will begin to break down the foundation of any community. In an atmosphere of mistrust—aggression and exploitation take over. In an atmosphere of trust and well-being—sympathy, compassion, and cooperation flourish.

Whenever you feel unsure about how you should respond to your children, what decisions to make concerning them, simply put yourself in their shoes. Feel what it's like to be them. Don't think about what is right for them, experience it for yourself. Even limit setting feels right when it is beneficial.

Teach your children the finer details of "doing unto others." Educate them not to hurt (physically or emotionally) themselves or anyone else. Do not allow them to be rude, exploitive, unkind, or destructive. Show them by example how to be patient, forgiving and understanding. (Use my booklet, *Teaching Children Values Through Storytelling* for help.) Treat your child the way you want her to treat you.

The biggest stumbling block for most parents is holding onto an old belief that they need to have an authoritative relationship with their children in order to have the power to control and mold them into the people they want them to become. Parents have been mistakenly led to believe that their children need to fear their disapproval in order to have their respect. Nothing could be farther from the truth. Fear only encourages our children to engage in protective behaviors. If they experience too much fear, discomfort and mistrust—anger, avoidance, and revenge become activated. The response is automatic; they are programmed to protect themselves. If you want your child to be open to your guidance then don't shut him down with your anger and shaming criticism.

You are your child's model. You could have no greater authority. Children watch the parents' every move and carefully mouth their words. Parents are the blueprint from which their children are building their lives; that's a given.

Your greatest challenge as a parent today is not to create a need for your children to defend themselves from you or the world, but to keep their trust intact. Your job is to show your child how to love, how to respect others, and how to better the world.

Our families, our towns, our countries, our living ecosystems, are based on interdependence. We are all connected. Those connections need to be nourished. The golden rule is not just some abstract moral code. It is at the core of our ability to survive and thrive as a species. And it starts the first day of life. Do unto your children as you would have them do unto you.

Appendix

Parenting Based On

	Authority	A Secure Bond
The principles at work	Obedience and compliance. Parental authority is based on being in control of a child's resources.	Providing for a child's essential needs and modeling responsive, respectful, cooperative, and empathetic behavior.
The way it's done	Controlling a child's experience of pleasure and pain. Instilling shame as a means of self-control.	Providing consistent and responsive care. Setting limits around disrespectful, unkind, and dangerous behaviors.
What baby learns	Cooperation based on obedience. How to use power to control the behavior of others.	How to treat others the way he or she has been treated—with empathy, respect and consideration.

Associations

LA LECHE LEAGUE
1400 Meacham
Schaumburg, IL 60173
1-800-LALECHE
708-519-7730

Will help you find local help. Much information on all aspects of mothering, especially breastfeeding. Very supportive. Will help you have a positive experience breastfeeding.

ATTACHMENT DISORDER PARENTS NETWORK
P.O. Box 18475
Boulder, CO 80308

Information and support. Has branches nationwide.

ATTACH
(Association for Training and Treatment in the Attachment of Children)
2775 Villa Creek #240
Dallas, TX 75234
214-247-2329

National organization

NURSING MOTHERS COUNCIL INC.
P.O. Box 50063
Palo Alto, CA 94303

Will provide phone counseling. Help you set up your own mothers' support group.

PREVENTION RESEARCH CENTER FOR FAMILY AND CHILD HEALTH
303 E. 17th Ave.
Suite 200
Denver, CO 80203
303-861-1715 ext. 225

Provides on-site support and instruction for low-income, first-time mothers and their babies.

F.E.M.A.L.E (Formerly Employed Mothers at the Leading Edge)
P.O. Box 31
Elmhurst, ILL. 60126

Chapters nationwide. A wonderful support system. Newsletter.

FAMILY RESOURCE COALITION
200 South Michigan Ave.
16th Floor
Chicago, IL. 60604
310-341-0900

Will help you to locate or start a family support group.

NATIONAL ASSOCIATION OF MOTHERS CENTERS
64 Division Ave.
Levittown, NY 11756
1-800-645-3828

How to locate or start a mothers center. Excellent for forming a support network.

PARENTS ANONYMOUS
675 Foothill Blvd., Suite 220
Claremont, CA 91711
909-621-6184

National network found in many towns and cities around the country. Education and support groups. Counseling for low-income families.

HEALTHY FAMILIES PARTNERSHIP
P.O. Box 69163
Hampton, VA 23669
1-800-884-6481

Hampton is the site of a very successful program whose focus was to support families better. The results have been phenomenal.

or

HEALTHY FAMILIES AMERICA
1-312-663-3520

They can help you to work toward creating greater support within your community.

KIDS FIRST
Box 5256
Airdrie, AB T4B 2B3
Canada
403-289-1440

Parenting workshops, resources, newsletter. Excellent organization. Penelope Leach and Burton White are on the board.

CANADIAN SOCIETY FOR PREVENTION OF CRUELTY TO CHILDREN
356 First Street
Box 700
Midland, Ontario, Canada L4R4P4

Information on prevention of child abuse. Has many FREE articles. See also Internet Resources.

DEPRESSION AFTER DELIVERY
P.O. Box1282
Morrisville, PA 19067
215-295-3994 • 1-800-944-4773

Education, support groups, newsletter.

FAMILIES SERVICE AMERICA
11700 W. Lake Park Dr.
Milwaukee, WI 53224
1-800-221-3726
414-359-1040

Provides counseling, information. Conducts research.

Magazines

MOTHERING MAGAZINE
P.O. Box 1690
Santa Fe, NM 87504-9780
1-800-827-1061

NURTURING PARENT MAGAZINE
373,918 16th Ave. N.W.
Calgary, Alberta
CANADA T2MOK3
403-870-4005

FAMILY CONNECTIONS
P.O. Box 782-CM
Radford,VA 24141

ADOPTIVE FAMILIES
2309 Como Ave.
St. Paul, MN 55208
800-372-3300

Articles and information for adoptive families, from medical issues to the challenges between siblings.

Newsletters

I suggest sending away for a complimentary copy to evaluate a newsletter in which you are interested. The subjects each newsletter covers will be apparent in the titles. The quality of the articles is something you will need to judge for yourself.

F.E.M.A.L.E. (Formerly Employed Mothers at the Leading Edge)
P.O. Box 31
Elmhurst, ILL. 60126

AT-HOME DAD
Peter Baylies
61 Brightwood Avenue
North Andover, MA 01845

KIDS
Box 5256
Airdrie, AB T4B 2B3
Canada
403-289-1440

SINGLE PARENTING IN THE NINETIES
6910 W. Brown Deer Road
Milwaukee, WI 53223
EMAIL: pilot pub@execp.com

DEPRESSION AFTER DELIVERY
P.O. Box1282
Morrisville, PA 19067
215-295-3994
1-800-944-4773

HOME BY CHOICE
P.O. Box 7734
Chandler, AZ 85246
602-857-3686

THE MOMS JOURNAL
Power River Communications
7046 SE Stella Court
Hillsboro, Oregon 97123
EMAIL: MOMISHOME@aol.com

SINGLE MOTHER
P.O. Box 58
Midland, NC 28107
704-888-2337

**RESOURCES FOR FAMILY DEVELOPMENT–
AND CHILD CARE ISSUES**
Rhonda Cardwell
1520 Catalina Court
Livermore, CA 94550
510-455-5111

Hotlines

Nineline: 1-800-999-9999
24 hour a day help for any problem

Child Help Hotline: 1-800-422-4453

24-hour helpline for parents at risk of hurting their child.

National Domestic Violence Hotline: 1-800-799-7233

Drug Abuse Hotline: 1-800-662-4357

Support

The Attachment Center at Evergreen
(303) 674-1910

Intensive residential treatment. Uses holding technique, which has received mixed reviews. Some have found it to be very effective, but it's not for everybody.

Cascade Center for Human Growth
P.O. Box 1144
American Fork, UT 84003
801-229-2218

Human Passages
777 S. Wadsworth Building One, Suite 1005
Lakewood, CO 80226
303-914-9729

National Foundation for Depressive Illness: 1-800-248-4344

**National Clearinghouse for Family Support
and Children's Mental Health:** 1-800-628-1696

National Institute of Mental Health: 1-800-647-2642

National Resource Center for Health and Safety in Child Care:
1-800-598-KIDS

Guidelines and requirements for out-of-home care.

The Internet

NATIONAL PARENT INFORMATION NETWORK
http://ericps.ed.uiuc.edu./npin/respar.html

A host of online pamphlets on a wide range of subjects for all ages. Review of and links to numerous magazines and newsletters.

ADOPTIVE FAMILIES OF AMERICA
http://www.AdoptiveFam.org/

Online catalog, membership, other links for adoptive parents.

BABYHOOD
http://www.babyhood.com

Geared primarily toward infants. Many other links to sites concerning childcare, parenting, etc.

PARENTING RESOURCES
http://www.kcts.org/product/single/resource.htm

Many good parenting tips.

PARENTS WITHOUT PARTNERS ONLINE HOME PAGE
http://www.parentsplace.com/readroom/pwp/

Local chapter search, articles, events.

WHOLE FAMILY ATTACHMENT PARENTING ASSOCIATION
http:// members. tripod.com/~JudyArnell/index.html

Many wonderful articles, books, and links to other sites. Breastfeeding, discipline, education, and medical information, home businesses, and general parenting issues.

PARENTS AT HOME
http/www.iquest.com/~jsm/moms/index.html

A good place for support. Interactive discussion forum, online newsletter, money issues, and other links.

MOTHERSTUFF—ATTACHMENT PARENTING
http://www.teramonger.com/dwan/html/parent-attach.htm

Good resource for attachment parenting. Articles, tips, many other links.

PARENT SOUP

http://www,parentsoup.com

Online magazine and chat group.

LACTATION, BREASTFEEDING, INFANT NUTRITION

http://www.efin.org/~djz/birth/breastfeeding.html

Articles, newsgroups, other resources.

THE BREASTFEEDING PAGE

http://www.islandnet.com/~bedford/br-page2.html

Helpful information and tips on breastfeeding and sleep problems.

NURTURING PARENT

http://www.thenurturingparent.com/welcome-js.html

Excellent online magazine, archive of articles, plus wonderful feedback from other parents.

WORK AT HOME MOMS—(WAHM)

http://www. wahm.com/

Online newsletter and discussion group.

AWARE PARENTING INSTITUTE

http://www.sb.net/awarepar/

Online articles, consultations, links, books, and workshop announcements

ZERO TO THREE

http://www.zerotothree.org/index.html

National advocacy and information network. Many good articles. Very connected to policy makers in Washington.

MOTHERHOOD ADJUSTMENT SERVICES

e-mail: MAS@mindlink.bc.ca Julia Benton.

Counseling on phone, information. Great support network.

Online Listservers and Chat Lines

NURTURING PARENT

http://www.thenurturingparent.com/welcome-js.html

ATTACHMENT PARENTING
sah-ap-request@kjsl.com

PARENT SOUP
http://www.parentsoup.com

WORK AT HOME MOMS--(WAHM)
http://www. wahm.com/

PARENTS AT HOME
http/www.iquest.com/~jsm/moms/index.html

Work

INTERNATIONAL HOMEWORKERS ASSOCIATION
http://www.homeworkers.org/

NORTH AMERICAN SMALL BIZ ALLIANCE
http://www.isquare.com

AMERICAN WOMEN ECONOMIC DEVELOPMENT CORPORATION
1-800-222-2933

NATIONAL JOB CORPS INFO LINE (BILINGUAL)
1-800-733-5627

U.S. SMALL BUSINESS ADMINISTRATION
1-800-235-2732

CONSUMER CREDIT COUNSELING
1-800-388-2227

TELECOMMUTERS INFORMATION
1-301-963-0370

MAW/HOMEBASE-- For Women at Home
Department CM
P.O. Box 4104
Ottawa, Canada K1S5B1

CONNEXIONS
P.O. Box 1461
Manassas, VA 22110
703-791-6264

Quarterly newsletter for managing home-based businesses while raising children.

Suggested Reading

THE BABY BOOK: EVERYTHING YOU NEED TO KNOW ABOUT YOUR BABY—FROM BIRTH TO AGE TWO
and
PARENTING THE FUSSY BABY AND HIGH-NEED CHILD—FROM BIRTH TO AGE FIVE
By William Sears, M.D. and Martha Sears

IT TAKES A VILLAGE
By Hillary Rodham Clinton

ON BECOMING A FAMILY: THE GROWTH OF ATTACHMENT INFANTS AND MOTHERS
By T. Berry Brazelton

YOUR BABY AND CHILD: FROM BIRTH TO AGE FIVE
and
CHILDREN FIRST
By Penelope Leach

DON'T TOUCH MY HEART: HEALING THE PAIN OF THE UNATTACHED CHILD
By Lynda Gianforte Mansfield et al.

THE TEN GREATEST GIFTS I GIVE MY CHILDREN—PARENTING FROM THE HEART
By Steven W. Vannoy

100 THINGS YOU CAN DO TO KEEP YOUR FAMILY TOGETHER ... WHEN IT SEEMS LIKE THE WHOLE WORLD IS TRYING TO PULL IT APART
By Marge Kennedy

THE HURRIED CHILD
By David Elkind

BETWEEN FATHER AND CHILD: HOW TO BECOME THE FATHER YOU WANT TO BE
By Ronald Levant and John Kelly

FATHERS DAY: NOTES FROM A NEW DAD IN THE REAL WORLD
By Bill McCoy

DEPRESSION AFTER CHILDBIRTH: HOW TO RECOGNIZE, TREAT, AND PREVENT POSTPARTUM DEPRESSION
By Katharina Dalton and Wendy M. Holton

WOMANLY ART OF BREASTFEEDING
By La Leche League International

THE COMPLETE BOOK OF BREASTFEEDING
By Marvin S. Eiger and Sally Wendkos Olds

BEING THERE: THE BENEFITS OF A STAY-AT-HOME PARENT
By Isabelle Fox and Norman M. Lobsenz

GIVING THE LOVE THAT HEALS
By Harville Hendrix

CONFESSIONS OF A HAPPILY ORGANIZED FAMILY
By Denise Schofield

THE WORKING PARENTS HELP BOOK
By Susan Crites Price and Tom Price

CHILD CARE: A PARENTS GUIDE
By Sonja Flating

DIVORCE BUSTING: A REVOLUTIONARY AND RAPID PROGRAM FOR STAYING TOGETHER
By Michele Weiner-Davis

DISTANT PARTNER: HOW TO TEAR DOWN EMOTIONAL WALLS AND COMMUNICATE WITH YOUR HUSBAND
By Lee Carter

BABY MASSAGE—PARENT INFANT BONDING THROUGH TOUCH
By Amelia P. Auckett

BABY MASSAGE: A PRACTICAL GUIDE TO MASSAGE AND MOVEMENT FOR BABIES AND INFANTS
By Peter Walker

SIBLINGS WITHOUT RIVALRY
and
HOW TO TALK SO CHILDREN WILL LISTEN AND LISTEN SO CHILDREN WILL TALK
By Adel Faber and Elaine Mazlish
MAGICAL CHILD
and
EVOLUTION'S END: CLAIMING THE POTENTIAL OF OUR INTELLIGENCE
By Joseph Chilton Pearce

COMMUNITY MOBILIZATION: STRATEGIES TO SUPPORT YOUNG CHILDREN AND THEIR FAMILIES
By A. Dombro, N. Sazer O'Donnell, E. Galinsky, S.G. Melcher and A. Farber

RAISING KIDS WITH JUST A LITTLE CASH
By Lisa Reid

Selected Bibliography

Ainsworth, M.D.S., *Infancy in Uganda*. Baltimore, Maryland: John Hopkins University Press, 1967.

Belsky, J., Nezworski, T., *Clinical Implications of Attachment*. Hillsdale, New Jersey: Erlbaum, 1988.

Bornstein, M., (Ed.), *Maternal Responsiveness: Characteristics and Consequences*. (New Directions for Child Development Series) Number 43, Spring 1989. San Francisco, California: Jossey-Bass, Inc.,

Bowlby, J., *Attachment and Loss. Vol. 1: Attachment*. New York: Basic Books Inc., 1969.

Bowlby, J., *Attachment and Loss Vol. 2: Separation*. New York: Basic, 1973.

Bowlby, J., *Attachment and Loss Vol. 3: Loss, Sadness, and Depression*. New York. Basic, 1980

Brazelton, T.B., *On Becoming a Family: The Growth of Attachment*. New York: Delacorte Press, 1981.

Brazelton, T.B., *Working and Caring*. Reading, Massachusetts: Addison-Wesley, 1985.

Brazelton, T.B., *What Every Baby Knows*. Reading, Massachusetts: Addison-Wesley, 1987.

Brazelton, T.B., Cramer, B.G., *The Earliest Relationship*. Reading, Massachusetts: Addison-Wesley Publishing Co., 1990.

Brazelton, T.B., *Infants And Mothers*. New York: Delacorte Press, 1983.

Cline, F.W., *Conscienceless Acts Societal Mayhem*. Golden, Colorado: Love and Logic Press, 1995.

Colin, V., *Human Attachment*. Philadelphia, Pennsylvania: Temple University Press, 1996.

Dugger, C.W., *A Boy in Search of Respect Discovers How to Kill.* The New York Times (May 15, 1994) 1.

Egeland, B., Hiester, M., *The Long-Term Consequences of Infant Daycare and Mother-Infant Attachment.* Child Development 66: 474-485, 1995.

Elium, D., Elium, J., *Raising A Son.* Hillsboro, Oregon: Beyond Words Publishing, 1992.

Erikson, E., *Childhood and Society.* New York: Norton, 1950.

Forbes, J., Weiss, D., *The Co-Sleeping Habits of Military Children.* Mil Med 157: 196-200.

Fromm, E., *The Sane Society.* New York: Holt, Rinehart, and Winston. 1955.

Garmezy, N., Rutter, M., (Eds.) *Stress, Coping, and Development in Children.* Baltimore: The John Hopkins University Press, 1988.

Goldberg, S., Muir, R., Kerr, J., (Eds.) *Attachment Theory: Social Developmental, and Clinical Perspectives.* Hillsdale, New Jersey: The Analytic Press, 1995.

Goldstein, A., *Violence In America.* Palo Alto, California: Davies-Black Publishing, 1996.

Goleman, D., *Emotional Intelligence.* New York: Bantam Books, 1995.

Green, R.G., *Human Aggression.* Pacific Grove, California: Brooks/Cole Publishing Company, 1990.

Greenspan, S., Greenspan, N.T., *First Feelings.* New York: Penguin Books, 1985.

Hart, A.D., *Stress and Your Child: Know the Signs and Prevent the Harm.* Dallas, Texas: Word Publishing, 1992.

Harwood, R.L., Miller, J.G., Irizarry, N.L., *Culture And Attachment.* New York: Guilford Press, 1995.

Haveman, R., Wolfe, B., *Succeeding Generations*. New York: Russell Sage Foundation, 1995.

Hefler, R.E., Kempe, R.S. *The Battered Child*. Chicago: The University of Chicago Press, 1987.

Herman, J. L., Perry, J. C., van der Kolk, B. A., *Childhood Origins of Self-Destructive Behavior*. American Journal of Psychiatry 148: 1665-1670, 1991.

Howes, C., Rodning, C., Galluzzo, D.C., Myers, L., *Attachment and Child Care: Relationships with Mother and Caregiver*. Early Childhood Research Quarterly. 3: 403-416, 1988.

Hunter, B., *Storm Clouds or a Drizzle? A Look at a New Study on Child Care*. Paper for Family Research Council.

Karen, R., *Becoming Attached*. The Atlantic Monthly February: 65-67, 1990.

Karen, R., *Becoming Attached*. New York: Warner Books, 1994.

Klaus, M.H., Leger,T., Trause, A., (Eds.) *Maternal Attachment and Mothering Disorders*. Skillman, N.J.: Johnson and Johnson, 1982.

Leach, P., *The First Six Months: Getting Together With Your Baby*. New York: Alfred A. Knopf,1987.

Leach, P., *Children First*. New York: Vintage Books, 1995.

Lewis, M., Worobey, J.,(editors) *Infant Stress And Coping*. San Francisco, California: Jossey-Bass Inc. Publishers, Number 45, Fall 1989.

Liedloff, J., *The Continuum Concept*. Reading, Massachusetts: Addison-Wesley,1985.

Lorenz, C., *On Aggression*. New York: Harcourt Brace Javanovich, 1963.

Magid, K., McKelvey, C.A., *High Risk: Children Without A Conscience*. New York: Bantam Books, 1989.

Maslow, A.H., *The Farthest Reaches of Nature*. New York: Penguin Books, 1971.

Mason,D., Ingersoll,D., *Breastfeeding And The Working Mother*. New York: St. Martin's Press, 1986.

McKenna, J., Mosko, S., Richard, C., *Bedsharing Promotes Breastfeeding*. Pediatrics 100: 214-219, 1997.

McKenna, J., Mosko, S., Richard, C., *et al, Experimental Studies of Infant-Parent Co-sleeping: Mutual Physiological and Behavioral Influences and their relevance to SIDS (Sudden Infant Death Syndrome)*. Early Human Development 38: 187-201, 1994.

Miller, A., *For Your Own Good: Hidden Cruelty in Child-rearing and the Roots of Violence*. New York: Farrar, Straus, Giroux, 1989.

Montagu, A., *Culture and Human Development*. London: Prentice-Hall, 1974.

Montagu, A., *Touching: The Human Significance of the Skin*. Perennial Library, 1986.

Mosko, S., Richard, C., McKenna, J., *Maternal Sleep and Arousals During Bedsharing with Infants*. American Sleep Disorder Association and Sleep Research Society 20: 142-150, 1997.

Mosko, S., Richard, C., McKenna, J., *Infant Arousals During Mother-Infant Bed Sharing: Implications for Infant Sleep and Sudden Infant Death Syndrome Research*. Pediatrics 100: 841-849, 1997.

Myers, D., *The Pursuit of Happiness*. New York: Avon Books, 1992.

Nesse, R. M., *An Evolutionary Perspective on Substance Abuse*. Ethology and Sociobiology 15 (1994) 339-348.

Nesse, R. M., Williams, G.C., *Why We Get Sick*. New York: Vintage Books, 1994.

Pearce, J.C., *The Magical Child*. New York: Bantam Books, 1980.

Pearce, J.C., *Evolutions End*. San Francisco, California: Harper San Francisco,1993.

Plutchik, R., *A Psychoevolutionary Theory of Emotions*. Social Science Information 21: 529-553, 1982.

Plutchik, R., *The Psychology and Biology of Emotion*. New York: HarperCollins, 1994.

Plutchik, R., Kellerman, H., *The Theories of Emotion, Vol. 1*. Orlando, F., Restak, R., Brainscapes. New York: Hyperion, 1995.

Peyser, M., Underwood, A., *Nature or Nurture*. Newsweek Special Edition, (Spring/Summer 1997) 60-63.

Reber, K., *Children at Risk for Reactive Attachment Disorder: Assessment, Diagnosis and Treatment*. Progress: Family Systems Research and Therapy, Phillips Graduate Institute, Encino, CA, Volume 5: 83-98, 1996.

Restak, R., *Brainscapes*. New York: Hyperion, 1995.

Sears, W., Sears, M., *The Baby Book*. Boston: Little Brown and Comp., 1993.

Stoufe, L.A., *Emotional Development*. New York: Cambridge University Press, 1996.

Spock, B., *Baby and Child Care*. New York: Pocket Books,1970.

Watkins, K.P., *Parent Child Attachment*. New York: Garland Publishing, 1987.

Wilson, E.O., *In Search of Nature*. Washington, DC: Island Press, 1996.

Wilson, E.O., *Sociobiology*. Cambridge, Massachusetts: Harvard University Press, 1975.

Wright, R., *The Moral Animal*. New York: Pantheon Books, 1994.

Index

addictions and 127

bonding 122–126

evolutionary design 119–121

intuition 65

mother taking charge and 123–124

need for support 122

practical suggestions for 126–127

stay-at-home 26

Fight or flight 18, 120

G

Gay parents 125

Genes 17

gene pool 197

Genetic coding 119, 121, 150, 198

Genetic memory 93

Genetic programming 16–18, 20–22, 32, 34, 82, 93, 97, 111

Genetic weakness 43

Greenspan, Stanley 31

Gunner, Megan 15

Guns

children killed by 181

in schools 181

H

Health

physiological 8, 10, 11, 19, 176

psychological 10, 11

Hormones

adrenaline 17

cortisol 15, 183

growth, in newborn animals 18

in breast milk 77, 96

oxytocin 26, 164, 176

post partum depression 176

progesterone 77

prolactin 26, 176

released during birth 8

stress 16, 18

that promote feelings of attachment 20, 164

tranquilizing 8, 20, 71, 76

I

I Am Your Child 41

Imaging scans 13, 15

Independence. See Autonomy

Infant

asylums and orphanages 43

autonomy 21, 110–112

brain development 13–16

carriers 85–87

common discomforts 65–67

cycles of waking and sleep 62

early experiences, effects on 14

effects of labor 8

effects of not being held 11

evolution 17–19

healthy development of 23

hospitalized 166–167

inadequate care, effects of 28

inherited systems for survival 19–23

massage 67

primary mode of learning 28

soothing devices, use of 85

training of 84

Infant, basic needs 11, 46, 92

Infant behavior 28

acting out 107–108

clingy 30

definition of undesirable 46

dysfunctional 46

Acknowledgements

This book would not have been possible without the love and support of my family and the friends I have had over the years. A special thanks to my husband, Jack, my true love and best friend, and our two wonderful children, Matt and Alex, whose love has healed my heart. To Vinnie for showing me how to be a good mother. To Lexie, Leslie, Robin, Alice, Toni, Martha, Betty, Betti, Lorien and Janna for their support. To Paul and Tamra—for providing the nest in which this book emerged. To Foster Cline, Harville Hendrix, James McKenna, Curt Matthews, Stanley Greenspan and William Sears for their important feedback and contributions. To my husband, Jack, for his enormous help with everything. To my patient and talented designer, Lewis Agrell. To Kathryn Agrell, Ann Jerlow, Ellen Kemper, Lexie Curtis and Sharon Franco for their tremendous help in getting this book finished. To the members of Arizona Book Publishers Association and Publishers Marketing Association for all their support.

Other Titles From

Teaching Values Through Storytelling
Disciplining Your Small Child
Eight Steps to a Better Marriage

Fax orders: (520) 636-9556

Phone orders: Call TOLL FREE: 1 (800) 966-0325

E-Mail orders: cocoon@primenet.com

Postal orders: Cocoon Books

        303 E. Gurley St., Suite 206

        Prescott, AZ 86301

Customer Service: (520) 636-9626